Everything
School Leaders
Need to Know About
ASSESSMENT

For Sarah
Who, as a former elementary and middle school principal, was precisely the kind of school leader for whom this book was written.

W. JAMES POPHAM

Everything School Leaders
Need to Know About
ASSESSMENT

CORWIN
A SAGE Company

For information:

Corwin
A SAGE Company
2455 Teller Road
Thousand Oaks, California 91320
(800) 233–9936
Fax: (800) 417–2466
www.corwin.com

SAGE Ltd.
1 Oliver's Yard
55 City Road
London EC1Y 1SP
United Kingdom

SAGE India Pvt. Ltd.
B 1/I 1 Mohan Cooperative
    Industrial Area
Mathura Road,
New Delhi 110 044
India

SAGE Asia-Pacific Pte. Ltd.
33 Pekin Street #02-01
Far East Square
Singapore 048763

Printed in the United States of America

Library of Congress Cataloging-in-Publication Data

Popham, W. James.
    Everything school leaders need to know about assessment / W. James Popham.
        p. cm.
Includes bibliographical references and index.
ISBN 978-1-4129-7979-5 (pbk.)
    1. Educational evaluation. 2. Educational leadership. I. Title.

LB2822.75.P67 2010
371.26—dc22   2009054004

This book is printed on acid-free paper.

10 11 12 13 14 10 9 8 7 6 5 4 3 2 1

Acquisitions Editor:	Arnis Burvikovs
Associate Editor:	Desirée A. Bartlett
Editorial Assistants:	Kimberly Greenberg and Joanna Coelho
Production Editor:	Eric Garner
Copy Editor:	Adam Dunham
Typesetter:	C&M Digitals (P) Ltd.
Proofreader:	Joyce Li
Indexer:	Jean Casalegno
Cover Designer:	Michael Dubowe

Contents

List of Tables and Figures

Preface

"It is better to know than not to know." This adage, as is the case with all such adages, conveys a commonly recognized reality. Although we can understand why, in rare instances, someone might prefer to remain unaware of certain kinds of knowledge, it is almost always better to be knowledgeable than to be unknowledgeable—even when the knowledge involved might be unpleasant.

For today's school leaders to be unknowledgeable about educational assessment is more than professionally imprudent: It is professionally suicidal. Students' test scores have become the yardsticks by which the people who operate our schools are judged. Thus, school leaders who know naught about assessment are heading into battle without important protective armor. School leaders who know naught about assessment are nutty.

And this is precisely the reason I wrote this book. I wanted to support those who run our schools by helping them understand what they truly *need to know* about educational assessment. Frankly, I don't think there are any books currently available that accomplish such a mission very well. Most of the assessment books written for educators enshroud their messages in off-putting quantitative complexities. Moreover, many of those books deal with nice-to-know, not need-to-know, content. In contrast, I've tried in this book to avoid the use of quantitatively rooted explanations, and I've been ruthless in deciding what it is that school leaders genuinely *must* know about educational assessment.

First off, let me tell you precisely for whom I wrote the book. After all, you may be holding the wrong book here. Once I've identified the intended audience for the book, I'll set forth more specifically what the book's mission is. Then you can decide if this is the right book for you.

WHO IS A SCHOOL LEADER?

As this book's title indicates, it was written for school leaders. But who are these school leaders? To me, a school leader is any educator whose routine responsibilities call for improving a school's instructional success. Among those individuals would surely be a school's principal and, if a school is large enough, any assistant principals. Also included would be those district administrators whose decisions often play an important role in the performance of every school in a district. In short, I'd regard just about any educational administrator, whether functioning at the school, district, state, or provincial levels, as a bona fide school leader. Those folks are supposed to be improving the quality of schools for which they're responsible.

But what about teachers? Can classroom teachers also be school leaders? Well, I certainly think so—but only in certain instances. I believe teachers are school leaders *when those teachers contribute to the educational effectiveness of their teacher colleagues.* For example, a fourth-grade teacher who creates a year-long teacher-learning community in her school so some of the school's teachers could more effectively differentiate their own instructional activities should surely be regarded as a school leader. So would a middle school English teacher who supplies monthly e-mail suggestions to all of his school's teachers regarding how best to get teenagers to read with greater comprehension *and pleasure.* In short, not only should all educational administrators be considered school leaders, but the label of school leader should also be properly pinned on any classroom teacher who's trying to improve a school's curriculum, its instruction, or the evaluation procedures used in that school.

A Preoccupation with "Understanding"

I've written books about educational assessment in the past. Most of those were fairly traditional textbooks, the kind used in a graduate course such as "educational tests and measurements." There is a need for such books, and I confess that I've picked up several serious royalty checks from having written those sorts of measurement textbooks. But this is not a book written for such a course. No, this is a book written specifically for educational leaders who want to learn what they truly need to know about the assessment concepts likely to intrude on their professional lives.

I have not written this book to teach readers how to *perform* assessment-related procedures, such as actually computing a reliability coefficient or carrying out a real-life alignment study to match a test's content with a set of curricular goals. For those readers who want to become adept at carrying out such procedures, I'll point out where this sort of information can be obtained. But the focus of this book is exclusively on a reader's *understanding* the nature of the assessment concepts and procedures described herein. Surgeons who repair their patients' malfunctioning organs need not perform, in person, their own preoperation laboratory tests; but they surely must understand what the results of those tests signify. Similarly, school leaders need not build and administer classroom assessments or large-scale accountability tests, but they must understand, at least in general terms, how those sorts of tests are built and what their results signify.

So, if you are looking for a book that will help you discover how to actually carry out a host of assessment-related procedures, put this book down and grab another. My intention here is to describe such assessment procedures *only* as a way of helping you gain an intuitive understanding of how those procedures work. The push in the pages that follow will be to help you grasp the essence of what's going on when important educational assessment operations take place.

Indeed, at the close of each chapter, I'll lay out the most important notions associated with that chapter's content in the form of Crucial Understandings. An understanding that's *crucial*, according to my dictionary, is one "of vital or critical importance," and each chapter will end up with its very own small set of Crucial Understandings. As you read the book, I certainly hope you'll pick up other assessment-related understandings along the way, but if you "own" the Crucial Understandings in the book's first nine chapters, you'll definitely know what a competent school leader truly needs to know about educational assessment.

Also at the end of each chapter, you'll find a *very small* handful of Recommended Reading suggestions. At the close of the entire book, you'll find a complete compilation of these end-of-chapter suggestions in the Recommended Reading Roundup. The Roundup presents complete bibliographic information for all of the chapters' recommended readings along with a brief annotation for each of the recommendations. If you wish to follow up on any of the end-of-chapter suggestions, a quick scan of the relevant annotations should enable you to decide whether to tackle any of the end-of-chapter recommendations.

COMMUNICABLE UNDERSTANDINGS

Okay, so the book will be trying to get you to understand what's most important about a series of educational-assessment concepts and procedures. I hope such an aspiration makes sense to you. Nevertheless, we currently live in an era when a school leader's attainment of such understandings—all by itself—just isn't enough! That's because a variety of groups also need to understand much more than they currently do about educational assessment. I'm thinking specifically of parents, educational policymakers, laypeople, and even students themselves. Today's school leaders who understand educational assessment, therefore, have an important additional responsibility—and that responsibility is to relay relevant assessment-related understandings to those who, like themselves, need such understandings.

Let me illustrate. Please imagine that you happen to be a district associate superintendent, and your district's students have just earned a set of so-so scores on your state's annual accountability tests. Does this mean your district's schools are doing a rotten instructional job? An editorial in the local newspaper entitled, "Our Shoddy Schools," might assert this is precisely what's going on. But what if the nature of your state's accountability tests makes students' scores on those tests more dependent on the socioeconomic composition of the district's students than on the effectiveness with which those students have been taught? In short, what may be going on in this fictional situation could be a function of inappropriate state-level accountability tests rather than a reflection of ineffectual instruction.

Remembering that you are still an imaginary associate superintendent, what you need to be able to do is communicate to your district's citizens, and particularly to the parents of your district's students, *why it is* that the district's scores on the state test may be an inaccurate indicator of how well the district's students are actually being taught. In other words, you *personally* need to understand key concepts about the appropriateness of accountability tests well enough to explain those concepts to relevant constituencies—in a manner so that those other groups will understand what they need to understand.

So, in a very real sense, what is being sought from you by this book is a sort of "understanding-plus," that is, a higher-than-usual level of understanding. What the book aspires for you to attain is a level of understanding that permits you to effectively communicate what you know about assessment to those individuals who, themselves, have a stake in the many assessment-linked decisions that seem to almost surround our schools.

When you have finished the book's first nine chapters, in Chapter 10 you can quickly review its entire set of per-chapter Crucial Understandings. If you are able to relay at least a general understanding of those understandings to others, then this will make you a successful reader and, of course, will make me a successful writer. As you move through the book, therefore, try to comprehend what you're reading at a deeper level than you might ordinarily bring to a typical professional-development book. The understandings you will acquire in the following pages, if you are a true school leader, will not be for you alone. You must, indeed, comprehend these assessment understandings not only for yourself but also for others. School leadership has its distinctive responsibilities, one of which is for school leaders to elevate the levels of assessment-related understandings of those around them.

Today's educators, and especially our school leaders, are buffeted almost daily by issues linked to educational assessment. School leaders need to know such stuff. I desperately hope this book helps you to do just that.

—W. J. P.
January 2010

Acknowledgments

I am grateful to my Corwin editor, Arnis Burvikovs, with whom I have worked for many years and who pestered me relentlessly for the last few of those years to tackle this book. I am also indebted to my friend and word-processor nonpareil, Dolly Bulquerin, who helped me put the manuscript into a form that Arnis would accept.

Additionally, Corwin gratefully acknowledges the following peer reviewers for their editorial insight and guidance:

Kenneth Arndt
Superintendent
C.U.S.D. # 300 Schools
Carpentersville, IL

Marie Blum
Superintendent
Canaseraga Central School District
Canaseraga, NY

Robert Frick
Superintendent of Schools
Lampeter-Strasburg School District
Lampeter, PA

About the Author

 **W. James Popham**, professor emeritus at University of California Graduate School of Education and Information Studies, has spent the bulk of his educational career as a teacher. His first teaching assignment, for example, was in a small eastern Oregon high school where he taught English and social studies while serving as yearbook adviser, class sponsor, and unpaid tennis coach. That recompense meshed ideally with the quality of his coaching.

Most of Dr. Popham's teaching career took place at UCLA where, for nearly 30 years, he taught courses in instructional methods for prospective teachers as well as courses in evaluation and measurement for graduate students. At UCLA, he won several distinguished teaching awards. In January 2000, he was recognized by *UCLA Today* as one of UCLA's top 20 professors of the 20th century. (He notes that the 20th century was a full-length century, unlike the current abbreviated one.) In 1991, he took early retirement from UCLA upon learning that emeritus professors received free parking.

Because at UCLA he was acutely aware of the perishability of professors who failed to publish, he spent his nonteaching hours affixing words to paper. The result: 30 books, 200 journal articles, 50 research reports, and 175 papers presented before research societies. Although not noted in his official vita, while at UCLA he also authored 1,426 grocery lists.

His most recent books are *Classroom Assessment: What Teachers Need to Know*, sixth edition (2011) and *Assessment for Educational Leaders* (2006), Allyn & Bacon; *The Truth About Testing* (2001), *Test Better, Teach Better* (2003), *Transformative Assessment* (2008), *Instruction That Measures Up* (2009), and *Transformative Assessment II: Applying the Process*; *America's "Failing" Schools* (2005) and *Mastering Assessment* (2006), Routledge; and *Unlearned Lessons* (2009) Harvard Education Press. He encourages purchase of these books because he regards their semiannual royalties as psychologically reassuring.

In 1978, Dr. Popham was elected to the presidency of the American Educational Research Association (AERA). He was also the founding editor of *Educational Evaluation and Policy Analysis*, a quarterly journal published by AERA. A Fellow of the Association, he has attended each year's AERA meeting since his first in 1958. He is inordinately compulsive.

In 1968, Dr. Popham established IOX Assessment Associates, an R&D group that formerly created statewide student achievement tests for a dozen states. He has personally passed all of those tests, largely because of his unlimited access to the tests' answer keys.

In 2002, the National Council on Measurement in Education presented him with its Award for Career Contributions to Educational Measurement. In 2006, he was awarded a Certificate of Recognition by the National Association of Test Directors. In 2009, he was appointed to be a board member of the National Assessment Governing Board. Dr. Popham's complete 44-page, single-spaced vita can be requested. It is really dull reading.

1

Why Do We Test?

Most of us who chose to become educators did so in order to help children learn the things they ought to learn. Typically, we started off by wanting to be teachers. Then, after we'd taught for a while, some of us decided to tackle other educational challenges, such as becoming school administrators. But the dominant motive for first selecting an educational career is almost always to help students learn. Let's face it, few people opt to become educators as part of a get-rich-quick financial strategy.

Okay, what is the nature of this "learning" we hope to promote in our students? Well, the things students ought to learn are, for the most part, skills and knowledge. The *skills* involved are usually intellectual skills, such as when students are able to compose a coherent essay. But children also need psychomotor skills, such as being able to use a computer's keyboard or discovering how to stay afloat while swimming. With respect to *knowledge*, there is a truly enormous collection of stuff that students need to know, for example, flocks of facts, tons of truths, and piles of principles. The more knowledgeable we can make students, the more likely it is those students can then employ their knowledge to deal with the world around them. If we can help students become both skillful *and* knowledgeable, of course, this will supply pretty potent support for those students' future success—and for their personal happiness.

However, beyond knowledge and skills, we should also be attentive to students' *affect,* that is, we should be attentive to students' attitudes, interests, and values. Because a student's affective dispositions can have an enormous impact on that student's life, educators who fail to promote appropriate affect for their students are falling down on a significant educational responsibility. We definitely want our students to learn how to read with comprehension, but we should also want them to *enjoy* reading. We definitely want our students to master mathematics, but we should also want them *not to fear* mathematics. So, in addition to promoting students' attainment of suitable skills or their mastery of needed knowledge, we should be also nurture students' acquisition of defensible affective dispositions. (Later, in Chapter 9, we'll consider ways that educators can assess students' affect.)

In a very real sense, then, education is organized so as to promote students' achievement of the three kinds of outcomes you see represented in Figure 1.1, namely, students' becoming more knowledgeable, more skilled, and in possession of life-enhancing affective dispositions. Admittedly, much more attention is currently given to promoting students' skills and knowledge than to promoting students' affect, and this will probably always be so. However, it may be helpful for you to recognize that, whether you are currently a classroom teacher or a school administrator, the overriding goal of the educational system in which you function is to promote students' attainment of what's in the three circles set forth in Figure 1.1. I find it difficult to conceive of any educational setting in which teachers should not at least *consider* the possibility of influencing students' knowledge, skills, and affect.

Figure 1.1 The Three Outcomes Educators Seek for Their Students

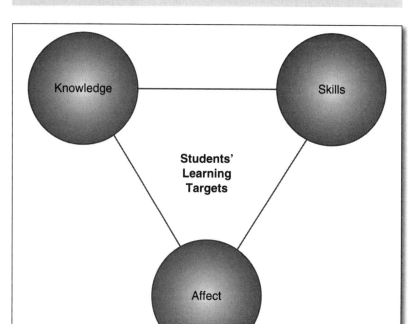

THE ROLE OF ASSESSMENT

If the mission of educators is to get students to end up with appropriate knowledge, skills, and affect, then where does assessment come in? Indeed, a fundamental question that all educational leaders should be able to answer—both clearly and concisely—is, *Why do we test students?* The current chapter is intended to help you answer this question. But, first, let me try to clarify a few potential terminology tangles that might, if not addressed, impede us.

In the remainder of the book, I will interchangeably employ the terms *test, assessment,* and *measurement.* Most of the time, I'll be using *assessment* because it appears to be the term most currently favored by educators. This is probably because *measurement* is a term seen as at least a little off putting, and when people use the word *test*, they often think of the sorts of traditional paper-and-pencil tests most of today's adults experienced when, as students ourselves, we went through school. Yet, especially in the last few years, we have been measuring students using considerably more diverse assessment procedures than represented by multiple-choice, true-false, and essay tests. Subtle definitional differences aside, however, when you understand the basic reason we "assess," "test," or "measure" students, you'll see that, regardless of which of these three labels is being employed, what's going on is pretty much the same thing.

As long as I've taken a short detour to do some terminology tightening, please allow me to clarify three more terms that will soon pop up in this chapter and will often be seen in later chapters. I'm referring to *curriculum, instruction,* and *evaluation.* You'll find that most educators understand what's meant by *instruction*—it's simply another label for *teaching.* And, *evaluation* is accurately thought by most educators to focus on how we determine the effectiveness of instruction, for instance, when teachers try to determine the quality of their own teaching. But there's a fair amount of confusion regarding the meaning of *curriculum.* Some educators think of curriculum as what is supposed to be learned by students; other educators regard curriculum as the materials used during instruction; and other educators think of curriculum as the actual activities that go on in class. Clearly, these definitions differ.

The way I'll be using the term *curriculum* in this book is as a label to describe educational *ends,* that is, the intended outcomes we want our students to achieve. Thus, the three types of learning targets seen in Figure 1.1, knowledge, skills, and affect, are all intended outcomes and, thus, can be thought of as *curricular aims,* that is, the skills, knowledge, and affect we aim for our students to attain. If curricular aims are the intended outcomes of education, then instruction (or, if you prefer, teaching) represents the *means* by which we intend to have students attain our chosen curricular ends. Along the way, we may wish to assess students during instruction to see if we need to make any changes in our current or immediately upcoming instructional activities. And once instruction is over—that is, when a sequence of instructional activities has been concluded—there is the need to evaluate the success of the instruction so we can determine whether to modify this instructional sequence when we use it again with future students.

As you will see, it is because of the need to make curricular, instructional, and evaluative *decisions* that educators assess their students. That's right; we don't test for the sheer joy of testing or because "it is interesting." Instead, we assess students in order to make better *decisions* about the curricular ends we should be pursuing, the way our instruction is working, and—at the close of instruction—how successfully students have achieved our intended curricular aims. Education is a decision-making enterprise, and educational measurement helps educators make better decisions. In short, we test our students so we can make more appropriate decisions about how to educate them.

COPING WITH THE COVERT

But there's a complication. We can't, by looking at kids, tell what they know. We can't, by looking at kids, tell what their skills are. We can't, by looking at kids, tell what their affective dispositions are. The reason we are unable to visually discern students' knowledge, skills, and affect is that all three of those things are *hidden* from view, that is, all three are *covert*. No matter how long you might look at a student who's sitting, perhaps only three feet in front of you, and no matter how intently and carefully you scrutinize this student, you simply cannot tell what's going on inside the student's skull. The student's knowledge, skills, and affect are quite invisible.

As indicated earlier, the entire educational enterprise revolves around educators' making appropriate curricular, instructional, and evaluative decisions. Yet, how can these decisions be made defensibly if educators have no idea about their students' *current* knowledge, skills, and affect? And this, of course, is where educational assessment comes roaring to the rescue—for it is through the use of assessment that educators can arrive at reasonable conclusions about such unseen variables as students' knowledge, skills, and affect. So, the answer to the Why do we test? question is that we employ test results to arrive at inferences—which we then use to make better decisions. Appropriate decisions enhance the quality of education we provide to students. And this is precisely the goal embraced by every school leader I've ever known, namely, to improve the quality of schooling provided to students.

For example, when students complete an information-focused quiz, then return it to the teacher, they are providing overt evidence about how much covert information they currently possess. Similarly, when students compose an original narrative essay as part of an annual statewide accountability test, they are also supplying overt evidence about their covert composition skills. And, when a classful of students complete an anonymous affective inventory indicating their current attitudes toward mathematics, they are also supplying overt evidence about the way they regard math.

When educators consider such overt evidence, they are then able to arrive at evidence-based *inferences* (or, if you prefer, they arrive at evidence-based *interpretations*) about educational variables that simply can't be seen. Assessment, in other words, permits educators to reach inferences about what's going on—unseen—inside the students who are being educated. Educational assessment, then, is fundamentally an inference-making enterprise. As you'll see in the next chapter, school leaders must understand that inferences are made by human beings and are not delivered ready-made, in cut-and-dried fashion by assessment instruments themselves. We'll dip into that important understanding when we look at what's called "assessment validity."

Curricular Decisions

But testing students, and figuring out what sorts of inferences must be made from test results, is not done without purpose. We do so to arrive at more suitable decisions regarding curriculum, instruction, and evaluation. To illustrate, let's look briefly at curricular decisions. It would be patently dull witted for educators to teach students stuff those students already know. By using appropriate assessment techniques, we can figure out what skills, knowledge, and affect a group of students actually possess when they initially come to us— thereby allowing us to avoid the serious curricular sin of trying to teach students what they've already learned.

Another set of curricular decisions depends directly on whether students possess the necessary precursive skills and knowledge so that a teacher's pursuit of particular curricular aims makes instructional sense. Without assessment, we can't tell if kids possess the requisite precursors. But by using educational assessment procedures, teachers can arrive at reasonable inferences about whether their students have the needed precursors before deciding to tackle specific curricular aims. Curricular choices made in the absence of assessment-elicited evidence about students' current status are curricular choices almost certain to be flawed. Defensible curricular decision making depends on the availability of assessment-generated evidence about students' current status.

Instructional Decisions

Turning to instruction, there are loads of instructional decisions that can be made more sensibly by relying on evidence regarding students' current status, for example, the degree to which students are making progress in mastering a challenging cognitive skill. If a teacher is deciding whether to spend more instructional time on a particular curricular aim and, if so, how to spend it wisely, these are decisions that can clearly be made more wisely when the teacher has evidence regarding how well the students have already learned what they are supposed to be learning.

Later, in Chapter 8, we'll take a careful look at a particularly powerful use of classroom-assessment evidence to improve teachers' instructional decision making when we consider *formative assessment*. But what should be clear to you already is that there are all sorts of teachers' instructional decisions to be made more astutely if only a teacher has access to assessment results enabling the teacher to arrive at sound inferences regarding students' current status.

Evaluative Decisions

Another prominent use of assessment evidence is seen when teachers set out to *evaluate* the success of this year's instructional procedures in order to decide whether to modify those procedures in the future when new students rumble into the classroom. Although we can regard this sort of assessment-abetted activity as exclusively evaluative rather than instructional, it should be evident that when teachers evaluate their teaching—with the prospect of fixing any flaws in it—this evaluative activity has all sorts of implications for subsequent instructional decisions.

Because, at bottom, we should evaluate the quality of instruction according to its payoff in changing students, there are numerous instances when those who evaluate instruction will have need for assessment evidence. You can't tell what changes have taken place inside students without collecting evidence about instruction's impact on a swarm of educationally relevant variables that we simply can't see.

The Multiple-Measures Myth

Any educator who has done a spot of serious thinking about assessment realizes there is peril in basing an inference about a student on only one test. Not surprisingly, therefore, during the last decade we have seen increasing numbers of educational policymakers calling for the use of "multiple measures" when making important decisions about individual students or groups of educators. It is thought, not unreasonably, that a solo indicator of quality will surely lead to defensible decisions. Indeed, the demand for multiple measures has become almost a measurement mantra for some educational organizations who rail against reliance on only one measuring device, especially when important outcomes are tied to students' test scores.

Let's remember, however, when we try to arrive at inferences about students' covert status, a single *good* measurement device is almost always better than four or five *bad* measurement devices. Simply adding additional evidence-gathering procedures does not ensure more appropriate inferences and decisions. Thus, when a school leader encounters a chorus of educators chanting for the use of multiple measures, the school leader should quickly pose the following question: What additional measures do you have in mind and, of course, how good are they?

Decisions, Decisions, Decisions

School leaders must understand, then, the only defensible reason for assessment of any sort is that it helps educators make better decisions about what to teach kids and how to teach them most effectively. Moreover, as you have seen, the evidence on whose basis these "better decisions" are made almost always requires the use of educational assessment.

Please consider Figure 1.2 for a moment. What you'll find depicted graphically is the way that the two mainstay operations of educational assessment—namely, assessing and inferring—are always the same, irrespective of whether the decision to be made is curricular, instructional, or evaluative. Let's look at what's going on in Figure 1.2.

Figure 1.2   Curricular, Instructional, and Evaluative Decision-Making Applications of Educational Assessment's Assess-Infer Essence

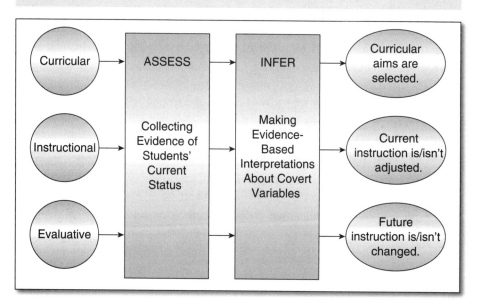

First off, please note the two center rectangles, identified as "Educational Assessment's Essence." As you can see in the rectangle at the left, this is when we actually assess students by using a potentially wide variety of measurement ploys such as formal paper-and-pencil tests or, perhaps, more innovative assessment procedures such as portfolio assessment. Then, in the right-hand rectangle, based on the overt evidence garnered from such measurement techniques, we arrive at inferences about the covert variables in which we are interested (such as students' knowledge of significant historical events or their algebraic skills). It is this *assess-infer* operation that we rely on to support a wide variety of educationally relevant decisions. This assess-infer process is, indeed, the essence of educational assessment.

Please look, then, at the three circles to the left in Figure 1.2 where you will see the most common decisions facing educators, that is, curricular, instructional, and evaluative decisions. A teacher's *curricular* decision might require an answer to a question such as, Which curricular aims should I pursue with this group of students? An *instructional* decision might hinge on answering the question, Do I need to make any adjustments in my ongoing instructional activities? And finally, an *evaluative* decision might call for an answer to a question such as, Should I change my just-completed instruction for my future students? Please note how you can see arrows from each circle indicating that, in order to arrive at a decision, the assess-infer process must be implemented. At the conclusion of this assess-infer process, the assessment-based inferences then contribute to the kinds of resultant decisions seen in the ovals at the right of Figure 1.2.

Clearly, there will be differences in the way educational assessment's two-step essence is applied in connection with the three kinds of decisions. For instance, when trying to choose curricular aims, the assessment to be employed would usually be regarded as a *preassessment* (or pretest) whose purpose is to get a fix on incoming students' entry knowledge, skills, or affective status. But when using the assessment process in order to make en route instructional decisions, a variety of short-duration and informal assessments might supply the evidence from which the teacher could arrive at appropriate inferences about students' progress. And, finally, for evaluative decisions about whether to make changes in a just-completed set of instructional activities—ones that will be offered in the future to new batches of students—a comprehensive and formal assessment approach may be warranted featuring the use of more expansive posttests.

But, as Figure 1.2 portrays the situation, no matter what sort of educational decision is to be made, the use of educational assessment's essence—that is, its two-step assess-and-infer process—provides the evidence-based inferences that allow educators to arrive at the decisions most apt to benefit students.

UNWARRANTED PERCEPTIONS OF PRECISION

Okay, now you've seen that educational assessment is essentially an inference-based tool to be used in the pursuit of improved educational decisions. This is a particularly profound truth—too often overlooked. Yet, once we have identified the proper use to which any tool should be put, this does not automatically indicate that the properly used tool is a terrific one. Even screwdrivers differ in their quality. The same is true of educational assessments.

If you'll agree that the underlying reason we assess students is to make better assessment-informed decisions about how to educate these students, there's a serious trap that, lurking out there, must be adroitly sidestepped. You need to dodge a perception that's held by far too many educators, namely, the fiercely flawed notion that educational tests are inordinately accurate. They aren't.

For the next few paragraphs, I'm going to be dealing with large-scale tests, such as the annual state-administered accountability assessments and the nationally standardized achievement tests educators have used for almost a century. These large-scale tests are the sorts of measurement devices most people—educators and noneducators alike—think simply ooze accuracy. In contrast, when we think of the classroom tests constructed by teachers, most people recognize that such teacher-made tests can vary substantially in their quality—and that certain classroom tests are surely substandard. But the "big tests" are usually thought to be particularly precise measuring sticks.

It's easy to understand why many educators and most citizens believe large-scale educational assessments are remarkably precise. After all, these important tests are developed by measurement organizations that have been doing this kind of test-construction work for ages. Indeed, the first U.S. nationally standardized achievement tests were published as far back as the early 1920s. You'd think, after more than eight decades of creating such tests, by now the folks who make these assessments would assuredly have gotten it right.

Then, too, there is the ways in which the results of educational tests are usually reported, that is, in a numerical—sometimes remarkably opaque—manner that simply reeks of precision. Indeed, today's test results are sometimes reported as numerical scores *with decimals*. What right-thinking person would dare challenge a decimal-anointed test score? Test results from large-scale tests seem so, well, precise!

Finally, because it is rare for the accuracy of educational assessments to be publically challenged except, perhaps, when a company scoring large-scale tests makes a major mistake, almost all people—including most educators—ascribe more accuracy and meaningfulness to today's test scores than is actually warranted. Thus, if you voice a position that educational test results are capable of yielding some seriously misleading results, you're apt to be seen as out of step with most of the populace. Widely held beliefs can sometimes entice new converts, and a belief that large-scale tests are super precise is sometimes a consequence of the prevalent view that significant educational tests are, indeed, quite accurate.

Most school leaders have surely observed students responding to significant educational tests. Because, in most instances, these tests are administered, scored, and interpreted in a carefully structured *standardized* fashion, those school leaders might conclude that the test results emerging from this standardized system reek of precision. But what's not immediately apparent is that, because most significant educational tests are intended to tap students' mastery of large numbers of skills and substantial bodies of knowledge, the folks who create these tests are forced to rely on items that, at best, can only *sample* those skills and bodies of knowledge. As a consequence, depending on how the item-sampled content of a specific test happens to mesh with a given student's prior instruction and idiosyncratic background, in any given set of, say, 30 students, you can be certain that the results are apt to be equivocal for many students.

Wishing Won't Make It So

Assessment specialists sometimes get bad-mouthed for crimes they don't commit. To illustrate, one of the most impossible tasks we've given to those who must create educational accountability assessments is assessing students' mastery of too many curricular aims. Just as an airplane cannot fly simultaneously at several altitude levels—it's impossible—educational tests cannot properly measure students' mastery of too many curricular aims—it's equally impossible.

Yet when the curricular specialists of a state or province decide on the curricular aims to be promoted by teachers—hence the curricular aims to be assessed by accountability tests—these well-intentioned folks almost always identify too many curricular targets. In short, members of these high-level curriculum committees tend to choose the many things that they *wish* their students would be able to do. Such choices often lead to an extensive wish list of curricular aims—too many to be taught in any depth during the instructional time available and too many to be tested appropriately during the testing time available.

As a consequence, because test-constructors must rely on a *sampling* strategy whereby only some of the officially approved curricular aims will be measured on a given year's test, and not with enough items to yield a

(Continued)

(Continued)

meaningful fix on a student's mastery of any assessed curricular aim, test developers are berated by educators because of their unpredictable, sample-based accountability tests. But, in this instance, we should be faulting the curriculum blokes—a bunch of blokes who yearned for too much.

Then too, we must remember such oft-cited causes for potentially misleading test performances by students as day-of-test sickness, inadequate sleep, or family distractions. Most people realize that, on a given day, a student may perform much worse on a test than if the test had been taken on another day. And some kids, of course, are notoriously poor test-takers, especially when a test is thought by those students to be significant.

But these widely recognized reasons for less-than-perfect test taking reside in the students, not in the test. What is definitely not widely recognized is that the tests themselves yield imprecise scores. Later in the book, we'll consider what measurement specialists call the "standard error of measurement." It's a way of quantifying the amount of *imprecision* that's apt to be encountered in a particular test. In many tests, even really important tests, the standard error of measurement is quite substantial, thereby indicating there's apt to be a substantial amount of looseness in a student's score.

The implication of the imprecision of educational assessment instruments is that, although less than flawlessly accurate, those tests will usually yield evidence that, interpreted cautiously, *will certainly be far better than no evidence at all.* But school leaders should definitely not ascribe unwarranted accuracy to even the most carefully devised educational assessments.

CRUCIAL UNDERSTANDINGS

All right, we've come to the close of Chapter 1, and it's time to focus on the most significant understandings you should have snared as you read the chapter. As noted in the Preface, you need to personally internalize these understandings sufficiently well so that, if necessary, you can explain them to others—particularly to your colleagues, to the parents of your students, to pertinent educational policymakers, and sometimes even to students themselves. So, after you've read a chapter's set of Crucial Understandings, please spend a few *extra* moments to consider how *you*, if you were required to do so, could get someone else to comprehend what's represented in each of those understandings. If you can successfully explain the nature of these understandings to others, you definitely will have understood what a school leader needs to understand about educational assessment.

A special collection of individuals to whom an astute school leader should give serious forethought are members of *the media*. Time and again, we see newspaper reporters who cover the local "education beat" truly mess up their stories about students' test performances. Distorted newspaper stories can, clearly, contaminate local policymakers' views about the effectiveness with which local educators are doing their jobs. So to minimize such distortions, school leaders need to remember one big-bopper lesson, namely, that *many media members who report on educational issues are astonishingly ignorant about educational assessment.*

Let me be candid. A newspaper's education beat is often given to journalists who are just getting under way with their careers, and we rarely see the reporters assigned to education stories choosing to remain for long in those posts. So, in general, we find a string of recent arrivals covering education events for local newspapers. And what these freshly minted education reporters usually know about educational testing will be what they recall from having taken tests while they were students themselves. So, unless a school leader gets remarkably lucky and finds a moxie, measurement-knowledgeable reporter covering local education stories, every school leader needs to do a proactive job in *educating* members of the media about any assessment-related issues germane to an upcoming story. Thus, as you find yourself trying to understand the notions treated in this book—and understand them well enough to explain those ideas to others—remember that a key collection of those "others" are members of the media who will be reporting on local students' test performances. Just imagine that you are trying to explain each of the book's crucial understandings to a greenhorn reporter who barely knows how to spell *test*. If you can, think through what a reporter would most likely be interested in, and try to put together a reporter-friendly explanation of the assessment topic you're treating. Assessment-informed members of the media will, most of the time, do a far better job for school leaders than will media representatives who regard the results of educational tests as having been divinely derived.

For this chapter, there are two key understandings, and they're set forth below. Note the use of atypical type. If something is really *crucial*, don't you really think it definitely deserves a bit of atypical treatment?

CRUCIAL UNDERSTANDINGS

- Educators use assessment-elicited evidence about students' covert knowledge, skills, and affect to make inferences that can then contribute to more defensible educational decisions.
- Although it is widely believed that large-scale educational tests are remarkably accurate, they are much less precise than is thought.

RECOMMENDED READING[*]

Dwyer, C. A. (Ed.). (2008). *The future of assessment: Shaping teaching and learning.* New York: Lawrence Erlbaum.

Reeves, D. (Ed.). (2007). *Ahead of the curve: The power of assessment to transform teaching and learning.* Bloomington, IN: Solution Tree.

Stobart, G. (2008). *Testing times: The uses and abuses of assessment.* New York: Routledge.

---

[*] Complete bibliographic information and brief annotations are supplied for the following recommendations in the Reading Recommendations Roundup (pp. 181–190).

2

Validity

Assessment's Cornerstone

One of the most widely misunderstood concepts in educational assessment is, strangely enough, the most important concept in educational assessment. Yes, most educators have a seriously mistaken idea about what's meant by assessment *validity*. Indeed, every time you find yourself in a conversation with colleagues during which you hear someone say, "a valid test," you can conclude you've spotted an educator who's confused about validity. When you've finished this chapter, you'll definitely be in a position not only to personally avoid conceptual confusion about validity but also to hopefully help others dodge such confusion. It's one of the longest of the book's 10 chapters, but it's definitely one of the most important.

THE VALIDITY OF INFERENCES

Okay, why is it such a vile mistake for someone to say, "a valid test"? Certainly, if you've been an educator for very long, you've surely heard this phrase voiced more than a few times by other educators. Well, here's the reason: It is not a test that is valid or invalid but, rather, it is a test-based *inference* that's valid or invalid. That's right, it's not the test; it's the inference.

You saw in the opening chapter that the fundamental reason educators test students is to arrive at inferences regarding those students' knowledge, skills, and affect. This is because each of those important educational variables is completely covert, that is, unseen. We give tests so students can respond *overtly* to those tests, for instance, by completing a true-false quiz or by delivering an assigned end-of-unit speech in an English class. Based on these overt performances, educators then arrive at inferences about a student's current status with respect to whatever covert variable being measured.

To illustrate, if an English teacher has assigned a series of extemporaneous speeches to students for the last couple of months, and for every such assignment the teacher has seen Jolene give a crackerjack speech, the teacher *infers* that Jolene is a competent presenter of extemporaneous speeches. Similarly, if Lamar's performance on his fourth-grade spelling tests is consistently inadequate, his teacher *infers* that Lamar's spelling skills are weak. We reach inferences about what we *can't* see in students on the basis of what we *can* see, namely, their overt performances on educational assessments. Clearly, if the tests we employ do not supply accurate evidence regarding students' unseen status, then we're likely to arrive at invalid inferences about students' status and, as a consequence, we'll probably make unsound educational decisions about those students. This is why assessment validity, with good reason, is regarded as the cornerstone of educational assessment. Valid inferences about students contribute to sensible decisions by educators about how to help those students; invalid inferences about students do the opposite.

All right, conceding that validity represents the central reason for which we test students, why is it so darned reprehensible for an educator to talk about "a valid test"? The answer to that question is simple: To the degree we think validity resides *in the test itself* rather than *in those who interpret* a test-taker's performance, we tend to ascribe validity to the test, not to the inference maker's judgment. As a result, we may think "a valid test" will invariably supply accurate evidence on which we can comfortably take action. What harm, after all, can come from a genuinely *valid* test? Inanimate tools, once identified as appropriate, are rarely questioned. When was the last time you heard a pair of pliers being maligned? So, once we start thinking of "valid tests," we may succumb to the belief that those wonderful assessment tools simply can do no wrong. Yet, it is *people* who make the inferences about the meaning of a student's test performance, and *people* can make mistakes—sometimes almost hourly.

School leaders must realize that, even with the very finest educational assessment devices, the inferences made on the basis of test-takers' scores are inferences made by human beings—human beings whose record for flaw-free thinking is far from impressive. School leaders dare not defer to test-based interpretations because those interpretations flow from "valid" tests. *There is no such thing as a valid test.*

In fairness, it must be conceded that when a person uses the phrase, "a valid test," this individual may actually be thinking that the inferences usually made when using the test are valid, not the test itself. So, if you're a school leader who, during a conversation with members of your local school board, overhears a board member utter the despicable phrase, "a valid test," I encourage you not to sneer visibly or to ask for the board member's resignation. Loose assessment language can occasionally be countenanced, especially from members of school boards.

COLLECTING VALIDITY EVIDENCE: THREE COINS IN THE FOUNTAIN

When I was growing up, "Three Coins in the Fountain" was both a popular song and a widely viewed film (starring

William Holden and Jennifer Jones). Well, when thinking about validity evidence, I often find myself humming that song, for there are definitely three decisively different kinds of evidence currently employed to support the validity of test-based inferences (or, you might also say, the validity of score-based inferences). We'll look at each of these three kinds of validity evidence in a moment, but first three preliminary considerations should be addressed.

First, whenever assessment validity is being discussed, it will be useful if school leaders can simply picture the following equation in their minds:

$$Assessment\ Validity = Inference\ Accuracy$$

You see, that's the essence of what the sometimes off-putting term *assessment validity* really signifies. When we say a test-based inference is valid, we mean the inference we've made, on the basis of a student's test performance, is *accurate*. If you can remember the simple little idea that "assessment validity equals inference accuracy," you'll be in good shape. And if you can remember that this validity (accuracy) applies to the test-based inferences made by sometimes error-prone people, not to the tests themselves, then you'll be in *great* shape.

Second, as a school leader, you need to know where these ideas about educational assessment actually come from so that, if anyone asks, without hesitation you can supply an on-target answer. For a number of years, the American Psychological Association (APA), the American Educational Research Association (AERA), and the National Council on Measurement in Education (NCME) have periodically published (about every decade or so) a collection of carefully crafted principles intended to guide those who create and use educational or psychological tests. The most current edition of those guidelines is called the *Standards for Educational and Psychological Testing*, and it was published in 1999 (American Educational Research Association, 1999). A new version is slated to be published fairly soon. Generally referred to in

measurement circles simply as the *Standards,* this set of pre-
cepts turns out to be quite influential, particularly in test-
related courtroom contests, because of the prominence of the
three sponsoring organizations and the typical prestige of the
representatives appointed by those organizations to put each
version of the *Standards* together. What you'll be reading in
this book is consonant with the most recent version of those
guidelines, but if you hear anything about a newly published
version of the *Standards,* please attempt to snare your own
copy, so you can see if any significant changes in major assessment concepts have taken place.

Third, and finally, the word *valid* is one of those terms
that's often used these days in a rather cavalier manner. We
hear about "valid political positions," "valid rationales," and
even "valid TV reality shows." One wonders whether, by definition, how unreal a TV reality show must be for it to be
regarded as invalid. However, *valid* has been transformed by
many people into simply a synonym for *good.* School leaders
need to remember that whenever they're playing in educational *assessment's* sandbox, *valid* means something quite specific. Moreover, the appropriate uses of this distinctive
concept should be governed by the interpretive conventions
invoked by relevant professional organizations, in this case,
AERA, APA, and NCME. If you're ever in doubt regarding a
technical question regarding educational measurement,
whether it refers to validity or any other assessment concept,
a quick trip to the *Standards* will usually prove rewarding.

What Makes a Test's Stakes High?

It is next to impossible these days for educators to watch a week go by
without at least one person's referring to some sort of "high-stakes test."
Many tests have, indeed, become the kinds of high-stakes assessment
instruments that, just a few decades ago, simply did not exist. But what is
meant, precisely, when we slap a "high-stakes" label on an educational test?

(Continued)

(Continued)

Well, it seems apparent that if the results of a student's performance on a test will have a direct impact on that student's life, the test should surely be regarded as a high-stakes assessment. For example, if a high school diploma is to be awarded (or denied) based on a student's performance on Test X, then it is clear that Test X should be seen as a high-stakes assessment.

However, it is also proper to regard as high stakes any tests whose results are seen to reflect the quality of educators' instructional performances. To illustrate, when an annual accountability test is administered in a state, and the results on this test are reported in the form of state-determined or federally defined performance levels (such as "proficient" or "basic"), then a school's results are apt to have an impact on at least some educational decisions in that school. Accordingly, such accountability assessments should surely be seen as high-stakes tests.

However, some tests, though not formally designated as accountability assessments, often influence public perceptions of educators' success. Accordingly, such tests should also be seen as high-stakes assessment instruments because students' performances on those tests usually influence educators' instructional decisions—in positive or negative ways. In short, any test whose results are likely to influence (1) *what happens to the test-takers* or (2) *what goes on in school* should definitely be regarded as a high-stakes test.

Let's turn, now, to a look at the three types of validity evidence currently sanctioned by the AERA-APA-NCME *Standards*. We will consider, in turn, three kinds of evidence bearing on the validity of test-based inferences, namely, *content-related evidence of validity*, *criterion-related evidence of validity*, and *construct-related evidence of validity*. As with what's treated in most of this book's chapters, if you wish to dig deeper into any of these three flavors of assessment validity, the Recommended Reading cited at the chapter's close will supply suitable shovels.

Content-Related Evidence of Validity

You'll note that this first of our three variations of validity evidence, as is the case with the other two, is described not as "content validity" but, rather, as "content-related *evidence* of validity." This seemingly innocuous verbal wrinkle in these labels is more significant than, at first blush, it might appear. You see, when measurement specialists try to support the validity of inferences derived from their tests, they don't simply carry out a solo study, and then proclaim a test does or doesn't permit valid inferences. On the contrary, what measurement folks attempt to do is build a *validity argument*, that is, an evidence-based argument that helps a test user determine how much confidence to place in the accuracy of inferences based on students' performances on a test. No single study, all by itself, will ever supply sufficient evidence of validity—nor should it. This is why almost all validation efforts associated with today's truly significant tests involve multiple evidence-gathering studies—studies aimed at supporting a solid validity argument.

Content-related evidence of validity indicates the degree to which an assessment satisfactorily represents the content domain being measured. In decades past, when the scrutiny of a test's "content" was first systematically undertaken, many of the early educational achievement tests were intended to measure students' knowledge of such factual content as dates and places of significant historical events. Because, for practical reasons, early test-makers could not assess students endlessly, those content-focused tests were obliged to *sample* the domain of content being assessed. For instance, if there were a spelling test intended to measure students' ability to spell correctly the words in a set of 500 "spelling terrors," the test-maker might try to sample the 500 words with a test containing only 30 or 40 items, then let a student's performance on that sample of words serve as a proxy for how the student would have dealt with the full 500 words. Given the various kinds of spelling principles present in the original 500 spelling terrors, the validity issue was, "Are the 500 original words adequately represented by the test's smaller number of words?" In the early days of standardized educational assessment, this issue was referred to as a *content-validity* question, and we sometimes hear people today still using the descriptive label, *content validity.*

But whereas early achievement tests were often composed chiefly of items that measured students' knowledge of memorized content, most of today's achievement tests put more emphasis on measuring a student's mastery of *skills,* that is, such cognitive skills as being able to identify critical flaws in the step-by-step description of a scientific experiment. Accordingly, when we see a study today collecting content-related evidence of validity, this study is almost always focusing on "content" in its broadest sense, that is, to include testing of students' cognitive skills as well as their knowledge of content in a more limited "memorized stuff" sense.

The chief way we collect content-related evidence of validity is *judgmental,* that is, by asking competent individuals to scrutinize the items on a test in order to judge whether whatever the test is measuring has been satisfactorily represented. That's right, *adequate representation* of whatever the test is measuring becomes the focus of any content-related validity study. Until a decade or so ago, here's the way we usually collected content-related evidence of validity. (Please wait just a moment and I'll describe more recent refinements of these earlier approaches.)

Traditionally, a content-related validity investigation typically started off by identifying the domain of content (that is, the knowledge and/or skills) supposedly represented by a test. In many instances today, what's being measured by an achievement test—especially by widely employed high-stakes accountability tests—is an estimate of a student's mastery of the curricular aims being assessed by the accountability test. These curricular aims might be called content standards, goals, objectives, expectations, benchmarks, or some synonymous descriptor. The challenge in early content-related validity studies was to secure the thoughtful judgments of qualified individuals regarding how well the particular set of curricular aims being assessed had been satisfactorily represented by a test's items. These judgments were collected and summarized then presented as content-related evidence of validity.

Typically, a group of, say, 30 experienced educators would be asked to take part in an item-by-item review of the items being considered for inclusion in a still-under-development test. After being oriented to their tasks, and having received suitable training to carry out those tasks, the reviewers were then given statements of the curricular aims being measured and an indication of the specific curricular aim that each item was chiefly intended to assess. Then the reviewers went through each item, signifying whether they believed a student's response to the item would contribute to a valid inference about the student's mastery of the curricular aim being measured by the item. The proportion of items judged by reviewers to have suitably helped measure their designated curricular aim was then recorded.

At this point, reviewers were asked to consider the *entire* set of curricular aims that the test is supposed to be assessing then indicate what proportion of those aims had been suitably addressed by the test's items. Ideally, all of the to-be-assessed curricular aims would have been satisfactorily represented by a test's items. Based on these two sets of judgments by the review group—that is, the on-target nature of each item and the overall representativeness of the curricular aims measured—a conclusion was then reached regarding the degree to which this study supported the validity of inferences based on students' scores on the test involved. Subsequently, when several similar studies had been conducted, a persuasive validity argument could then be fashioned.

More recently, because the explicit language of certain educational accountability legislation sometimes calls for tests to be "aligned" with official curricular aims, we have seen the emergence of numerous *alignment* studies. I'll now describe, briefly, some of the key elements of those studies. But what school leaders need to realize is that today's "alignment studies" are merely relabeled versions of yesteryears' content-validity investigations.

Among the most widely used of the procedures to study the alignment of accountability tests is the strategy devised by Norman Webb (2002) of the University of Wisconsin. Webb defines alignment as "the degree to which expectations and assessments are in agreement and serve in conjunction with one another to guide the system toward students learning what they are expected to know and do" (p. 2).

Webb set out to systematize the way educators could collect and analyze evidence to judge a test's alignment with its to-be-assessed curricular aims. Putting it a bit more precisely, a set of evaluative criteria were to be employed to determine whether a test satisfactorily assessed students' mastery of whatever curricular aims the test was supposed to be measuring. Rather than seeing these sorts of legislatively required alignment investigations be carried out haphazardly, Webb offered the four criteria presented in Table 2.1

Table 2.1   Webb's Four Alignment Criteria

Criteria	Focus
Categorical Concurrence	Are the same or consistent categories used in both the curricular aims and the assessment?
Depth-of-Knowledge Consistency	To what extent are the cognitive demands of curricular aims and the assessment identical?
Range-of-Knowledge Correspondence	Is the span of knowledge reflected in curricular aims and the assessment the same?
Balance of Representation	To what degree are different curricular aims given equal emphasis on the assessment?

and recommended not only ways of analyzing the resultant evidence but even suggested reasonable expectations regarding such evidence.

As you can see from Table 2.1, Webb's alignment strategy calls for those carrying out an alignment study to collect judgments from people who have become familiar with both the test under consideration and with the set of curricular aims the test was intended to measure. Typically, once a group of alignment reviewers has been assembled to review a test's items and the curricular aims it is supposed to be assessing, these reviewers are first trained in how to render the necessary judgments, then they are asked to supply ratings dealing with all four alignment criteria. For example, the depth-of-knowledge criterion focuses on whether the level of cognition embodied in the curricular aims appears to be matched by the cognitive demands of the items themselves. The criteria in Webb's approach constitute different dimensions, all of them relevant, for judging how well a test's content meshes with the curricular content it is supposed to be assessing.

Other approaches to the determination of alignment are also employed these days, but they all revolve around the central question of whether a test's items do a satisfactory job of determining how well a test-taker has achieved the curricular aims being assessed. Are any of these alignment methods perfect? As you might guess, this question gets a negative answer. Several of these alignment procedures stumble because the "grain size" of different curricular aims often varies. A curricular aim's *grain size* refers to the curricular aim's breadth of coverage. For instance, a curricular aim such as the following would represent a small grain size: "Students will be able to accurately add pairs of double-digit numbers." In contrast, a substantially larger grain size would be present in the following curricular aim: "Students will be able to accurately perform, for up through three-digit numbers, any of the following arithmetic operations: addition, subtraction, multiplication, or division." The grain size of any curricular aim is usually revealed by estimating the amount of instructional time it will require to get students to master the aim—larger grain-size goals take much longer to teach successfully than do smaller grain-size goals. Clearly, judging the alignment of large grain-size curricular aims to a given test's items might be substantially different than if an alignment study were focused on matching a test's items to small grain-size curricular aims. This is because fewer items are needed to satisfactorily represent students' achievement of small grain-size curricular aims. Yet, few of the available alignment methodologies deal suitably with these prevalent grain-size differences.

What school leaders must recognize about studies dealing with the content representativeness of educational assessments—whether those studies are called "alignment analyses" or "content-related evidence-of-validity investigations"—is that the most important consideration in such studies is invariably the *stringency of scrutiny.* That is, what's most significant in these investigations is the rigor of the analyses undertaken. I have personally seen many such studies carried out, and those studies definitely ranged in their analytic rigor. Some alignment studies are really demanding in the sense that a test's items assessing a given curricular aim must be "spot on" or those items will end up being judged as unaligned. Other alignment studies—far too many in my estimate—are remarkably relaxed, seemingly willing to regard an item as assessing a student's mastery of a curricular aim even if the item only remotely resides in the curricular aim's ballpark. What this signifies for school leaders is quite straightforward. You dare not trust an alignment's study's conclusions unless you have considered the procedures employed and, to your own satisfaction, decided those procedures are well conceived and, most of all, the procedures are *sufficiently rigorous.*

Content-related evidence of validity, the first of our three validity variations, is—far and away—the validity evidence most germane to the activities of school leaders. You need to understand, in at least a general way, how the other two sorts of validity evidence are conceptualized; but you need to understand far better how content-related evidence of variety is collected.

School leaders can also help teachers discover how they might go about collecting content-related evidence of validity for the more significant of their own teacher-made tests. Really, all that's involved is to simplify the approaches described in earlier paragraphs in such a way that teachers themselves can think about how representative their own tests are of the curricular aims those tests are supposed to represent. Teachers need to judge, perhaps informally, (1) whether each item in a test properly measures a student's mastery of the curricular aim the item is supposed to measure and (2) whether the complete set of curricular aims has been satisfactorily represented by a test's items. Even if this sort of activity were done only occasionally by teachers, and even for only their most significant tests, the beneficial impact of such analyses on the creation of teachers' future tests could be substantial.

Criterion-Related Evidence of Validity

The second kind of validity evidence to be considered is referred to as "criterion-related" because it is concerned exclusively with a test's ability to predict a test-taker's performance on some sort of criterion variable. The most common example of criterion-related evidence of validity occurs when we use students' performances on some kind of predictor test (such as the SAT and ACT, a pair of widely used college entrance exams) to predict how well those students will perform in college—as represented by the *criterion variable* of the students' college grade-point averages. Students take the SAT or ACT while in high school, and their scores on those exams are then employed to forecast the students' college grades. If high-scoring students (that is, those who earn high scores on the aptitude tests) also earn high grades in college, this is the sort of supportive evidence used in a criterion-related evidence-of-validity argument. As we saw in the case of content-related evidence of validity, a number of studies (not merely one) will typically be employed when building a powerful validity argument.

In Figure 2.1, you will see a graphic depiction of the typical nature of a study designed to collect criterion-related evidence of validity. First, we collect performance evidence from students on a predictor test, that is, a test whose measurement mission is to predict how well those who took the test will perform in some subsequent setting, usually an academic situation. The criterion variable is most often students' grade-point averages, but it could be any variable we wish to predict, for instance, students' subsequent job performance as reflected by their supervisors' ratings.

Typically, as seen in Figure 2.1, the predictor test is an academic *aptitude* test which, in contrast to the academic *achievement* tests intended to assess students' skills and knowledge, is deliberately designed to forecast a student's subsequent academic performance. Although the SAT and ACT are, by far, the two most widely used academic aptitude tests, for purposes of your understanding what's meant by this second kind of validity evidence (namely, criterion-related evidence), any kind of aptitude test will suffice. Early "aptitude" tests, incidentally, were built in the firm belief that children were born with certain inherited (largely "fixed") academic aptitudes, such as their verbal, quantitative, or spatial aptitudes, hence these sorts of predictor tests were understandably

Figure 2.1   The Typical Nature of a Study to Collect Criterion-Related Evidence of Validity

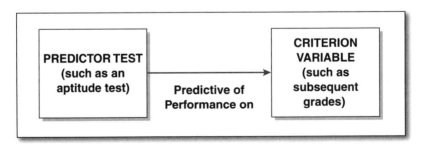

described as aptitude tests. In recent years, however, test makers have veered away from the use of the label *aptitude* because it tends to connote innate and truly intractable capacities on the part of students. Indeed, even the venerable *Scholastic Aptitude Test* that, since 1926 has been administered to hordes of students, is now officially called the SAT, thereby completely skirting the "aptitude" issue in its name. School leaders should know, however, because they may sometimes encounter the distinction between *aptitude* tests and *achievement* tests, this distinction is between a test built for predictions and a test built to assess what students have learned.

Rarely will school leaders be carrying out their own studies to secure criterion-related evidence of validity. But because some commercial firms will be trying to sell their assessments on the basis of such studies, school leaders need to understand generally how such investigations are structured. As you can see in Figure 2.1, there are two variables involved in these sorts of validity studies: (1) students' scores on the predictor test and (2) students' performances on the criterion variable. Typically, a simple correlation coefficient is computed to signify the relationship between students' predictor-variable performances and their criterion-variable performances. For these studies to be useful, it is clearly important that the measurement of both of those two variables be as accurate as possible.

Here's an example drawn from recent real-world attempts to improve students' scores on the annual accountability tests being used to evaluate the effectiveness of educators' instruction. During recent years, many commercial test vendors have been selling (to districts, states, or provinces) so-called interim assessments by asserting that those assessments will be predictive of students' performances on end-of-year accountability tests. The interim tests are to be administered every few months, and students' performances on the tests are supposed to help educators spot those students who are likely to get low scores on the end-of-year accountability assessments. To make a decision to purchase such interim tests, however, an educational decision maker clearly needs to see compelling criterion-related evidence of validity. In this case, each time an interim test is administered, it is supposed to predict kids' scores on the "big" accountability test. Accordingly, the companies attempting to sell their interim tests need to supply evidence of the relationship between each interim test (the predictor test) and the accountability test (the criterion variable). Strong, positive correlations between those two variables suggest the interim tests are, as claimed, accurate predictors of students' scores on the accountability test. Weak correlations between the two variables indicate the interim tests aren't all that wonderful at predicting what they are supposed to be predicting.

One last definitional nicety needs to be trotted out about criterion-related evidence of validity, and it stems from *when* a predictor test is administered in relation to collection of criterion-variable data. Typically, the predictor test is given a year or two prior to the collection of criterion data. For instance, a college entrance exam might be administered to high school seniors, and then criterion-variable evidence could be collected—college students' freshman year grade-point averages—more than two full years later. This kind of approach produces what's referred to as *predictive* criterion-related evidence of validity.

But when a test is being created, the test developers sometimes don't have the luxury of waiting for a year or two. Accordingly, they administer both the predictor test and the criterion test at essentially the same time. To illustrate, suppose a brand new college-admission exam had been created for use during high school, and its developers were eager to immediately collect some criterion-related evidence of validity. They might ask a group of college freshman (nearing the end of their first year in college) to take the new test then correlate those students' college grade-point averages with the test (normally given only during high school) that they had taken only a short while earlier. This strategy for collecting validity evidence, clearly providing less compelling data to support validity arguments than results of a *predictive* study, provides what is referred to as *concurrent* criterion-related evidence of validity. But whether predictive or concurrent, the persuasiveness of any criterion-related evidence of validity study depends on the quality of the criterion variable, the circumstances in which the two sets of data were collected, and the effectiveness of the predictor test in doing its forecasting job.

Predictions That Maim

Ask any 10 adults who took the SAT or ACT, even decades ago, to tell you if they can recall what their scores were. For at least 9 of the 10 of the people asked, the answer will be an emphatic *yes*. People remember if they scored an 1140 on the SAT or earned a 33 on the ACT. One reason they remember these scores is because society regards performances on those two college-entrance exams as so terribly important. Most people think if students score really well on the SAT or ACT, those students are super smart and, thus, are "college material." Students who earn low or middling scores on these college-entrance exams, however, are seen to be destined for more menial roles in life—roles where college success isn't required. Because colleges and universities, with several notable exceptions, still reach admission decisions by relying heavily on SAT or ACT scores, it is not surprising that most members of our society perceive these scores to be somewhat sacred.

There's also some pretty impressive data showing that high school students' scores on either of these two entrance exams are definitely predictive of the grades those students will subsequently earn in college. Indeed, the correlations between (1) students' scores on either the SAT or ACT and (2) those students' college grades are, on average, about .50. Such correlation coefficients are large enough to be "statistically significant." Even so, here's where the validity story starts to sour.

In order to determine how much of one variable (in this instance, students' college grades) is accounted for by another variable (in this instance, students' scores on the SAT or ACT), one needs to *square* the correlation coefficient that links those two variables. In this case, we must multiply the correlation coefficient of .50 times itself and, as a result,

(Continued)

(Continued)

we end up with .25. What those "statistically significant" validity coefficients are telling us, therefore, is that 25 percent of students' college grades can be accounted for by students' scores on college entrance exams. *But this leaves 75 percent* of students' college performance being influenced by nontest factors such as *effort*. In comparison to the predictive power of students' scores on college-entrance exams, fully three times as much of a student's college grades are associated with variables other than test scores.

And yet, far too many parents and far too many educators allow students' college-entrance-exam scores to adversely influence their perceptions of children. A child whose SAT or ACT scores are not stellar may be regarded by the child's parents as less able than had been believed prior to a score envelope's being opened. Perceptions that a child has low ability can be transmitted to children, sometimes in subtle and sometimes in not-so-subtle ways, by both parents and teachers. Such perceptions are not only apt to be wrong, but for the students who are on the receiving end of them, such perceptions hurt—sometimes lastingly.

On the flip side of this scoring scenario, students who earn super-high scores on the SAT of ACT are sometime regarded by adults as so inherently able that their "smarts" will surely carry them successfully through life. Such youngsters can often be coddled into believing that, because of their test-ratified brightness, they really don't have to expend much effort to succeed. But, whether parents or teachers are the culprits, such no-effort-needed messages can stifle exceptionally bright children's attainment of their true potential.

When it comes to what contributes to children's future academic success, the ratio is three to one in favor of nontest factors over scores on college-entrance exams. School leaders need to understand that the SAT and ACT can be useful—but can also be harmful.

Construct-Related Evidence of Validity

The final kind of *Standards*-sanctioned validity evidence is regarded by many measurement experts as the most comprehensive of the three types, that is, they think construct-related evidence actually subsumes the other two types of validity evidence. Here, in a nutshell, is the essence of this often-misunderstood kind of validity evidence. It starts out with the recognition that the things we measure in education are really *hypothetical constructs,* that is, hypothesized variables. Because we literally cannot observe a student's mathematical competence, spelling ability, or self-esteem, we hypothetically posit the existence of those covert variables. The intention of a study intended to gather construct-related evidence of validity is twofold: (1) to demonstrate that the hypothesized construct actually exists and (2) to show the test that's currently under scrutiny does, in fact, accurately determine a test-taker's status with respect to the hypothetical construct.

There are several ways this kind of construct-related evidence is assembled, and I know of no school leaders who revel in doing *any* of these sorts of validity studies. But, just so you have a rough idea of how they are carried out, here are some examples of the three most commonly seen studies dealing with construct-related evidence of validity.

First off, there are *intervention studies* in which we see if students' scores on a test are predictably different after those students have received a particular intervention. To illustrate, if a test had been developed to measure students' "spatial adeptness" (a student's ability to solve various sorts of spatially rooted problems), the tests might be administered early during a summer session and then readministered after students had received an intensive five-week course on "how to think in spatial terms." The five-week course is, in this instance, the intervention. If post-intervention scores are substantially higher than the preintervention scores, this is solid validity evidence of a construct-related sort.

A second approach to collecting construct-related evidence is the use of *differential-population* studies. Using this strategy, we identify two groups who, based on the experiences or abilities of the people in the groups, are meaningfully different with regard to their possession of the hypothetical construct involved. Then, we administer the test we're studying to the two groups, so we can see if their performances confirm our prediction. To illustrate, if a new test had been devised to measure a student's "ability to think historically," we might administer the test to a group of college history majors and also to a group of college students who had taken no more than one college history class. We would predict that the history majors would earn much higher scores on the new test, and, if they actually do, this would be supportive construct-related evidence of validity.

The final, commonly used approach to construct-related evidence of validity involves the use of *related-measures* studies. In this procedure, assuming we are studying a newly developed test, other tests are identified that are either doing the same measurement job or doing a decidedly different measurement job. We then either administer the two supposedly similar tests or, in contrast, administer the two supposedly different tests, to the same individuals. Next, we see if the predicted positive or negative correlations are evidenced. To illustrate, if we had developed a brand new college-entrance exam, we might administer the new test to a group of students who has also recently completed the ACT then see if the two sets of scores (on the new test and on the ACT) are, as we predict, positively correlated.

Please note that in the previous example, the ACT was not "the criterion test." The criterion variable in these kinds of studies would be students' college grades. So, this is definitely not a case of criterion-related evidence of validity. Many educators, once they see that two tests have been correlated, immediately assume they are dealing with an instance of criterion-related evidence of validity. That's often not the case. If two like-mission tests are involved, there should be positive correlations between test-takers' scores. If two unlike-mission tests are involved, the correlations should be negative. But if there is there is *no* to-be-predicted criterion variable involved, these are instances of construct-related rather than criterion-related validity studies.

Construct-related evidence of validity, more than the other two kinds of validity evidence, makes vivid that what must be constructed is a *validity argument*. The three most common kinds of approaches have been identified here, namely, *intervention*, *differential population*, and *related-measures* investigations. But other approaches might well be employed depending on the nature of what's being measured, that is, depending on the nature of the *hypothesized construct* to be assessed. Remember, in educational assessment, almost all the things we try to measure are hypothesized constructs.

As you can see, because construct-related evidence of validity is focused on determining whether a test measures its covert variable well enough to permit accurate score-based inferences, this is why most measurement specialists believe that both content-related and criterion-related validity studies are subsumed under the broader category of construct-related validity evidence. That's because both content-related and criterion-related evidence of validity can contribute directly to any argument about whether a test appropriately measures the covert construct it is supposed to measure.

CRUCIAL UNDERSTANDINGS

All right, we're nearing the conclusion of our consideration of what, according to this chapter's title is the "cornerstone" of educational assessment. What, then, are the few crucial understandings that today's school leaders must possess about assessment validity?

Well, you've seen that validity must be focused on test-based inferences, not tests themselves. Moreover, you've seen that to determine how accurate an assessment-based inference is, we need to build validity arguments that become stronger as additional studies are conducted in support of the inferences to be made. Those two points, interestingly, translate into a requirement that validity arguments must be marshaled *for every type of test-based inference to be made*. Yes, a test might be created to accomplish Measurement Mission X, but then subsequently be used to support Measurement Mission Y. As a consequence of the test's two uses, validity arguments—based on empirical investigations or judgmental studies—must be carried out to support the inferences associated with *both* of those measurement missions.

For example, suppose an achievement test had been constructed to measure middle school students' achievement of certain state-approved curricular aims in social studies. Validity studies should definitely be carried out to help us know whether our test-based inferences about students' mastery of those aims are valid. Typically, we'd collect content-related evidence of validity for that purpose. However, after the new test had been in use for a year, suppose it was also designated to evaluate the effectiveness of social studies instruction in that same state's middle schools. In other words, the test was now to be used for accountability purposes, and score-based inferences were going to be made about how instructionally effective the social studies program was each middle school in the state.

Well, this second measurement mission of the new test is substantially different from the test's initial mission, and, as a consequence, additional validity evidence would need to be assembled—this time probably of the construct-related variety—to show that, on this social studies test, effectively taught students out-performed ineffectively taught students. The guiding idea in this instance, a principle confirmed in the APA-AERA-NCME *Standards,* is that for every different application of an educational test—because of this new usage—an additional validity argument (accompanied by one or more types of validity evidence) is necessary.

CRUCIAL UNDERSTANDINGS

- Three professionally sanctioned varieties of evidence are collected, depending on an educational test's measurement mission, to support the validity of test-based inferences—rather than the validity of the tests themselves.

> • Because most educational assessments are used to determine whether students have mastered a set of curricular aims, educators must be particularly attentive to the quality of any alignment studies supplying content-related evidence of validity.

RECOMMENDED READING[*]

American Educational Research Association. (1999). *Standards for educational and psychological testing*. Washington, DC: Author.

Linn, R. L., Miller, D., & Gronlund, N. E. (2008). *Measurement and assessment in teaching* (10th ed.). Upper Saddle River, NJ: Prentice-Hall/Merrill.

Webb, N. L. (2002). *Alignment study in language arts, mathematics, science, and social studies of state standards and assessment for four states*. Washington, DC: Council of Chief State School Officers.

---

[*] Complete bibliographic information and brief annotations are supplied for the following recommendations in the Reading Recommendations Roundup (pp. 181–190).

3

Test Reliability

Some things chum around together so often that it's hard to think of one without thinking of the other. For instance, if educators take part in a word-association game where, upon hearing a word, they must say the first word coming into their minds, the word *salt* almost always triggers a response of "pepper." Well, in educational assessment there are two concepts so tightly tied together that they function as the salt and pepper of testing. I'm referring to *validity*, which you considered in the previous chapter, and *reliability*, the focus of this chapter. Validity and reliability have been hanging around together for so many years that it's almost impossible to think of one of those concepts without having its pal pop into our minds. And this is why any school leader who wants to be truly assessment-literate must know what's involved when test reliability trots into view.

Although validity and reliability are best buddies, and are generally regarded as the most important concepts in educational measurement, they really function in a decidedly different manner. You saw in Chapter 2 that validity resides not in a test itself but, rather, applies to the accuracy of the inferences we base on students' test performances—thereby making it a clear-cut mistake for an educator to refer to "a valid test." In marked contrast, reliability *does* exist in the test itself, so it is altogether appropriate for an educator to say, "This test is reliable" or, "That test is unreliable."

In the previous chapter, school leaders were encouraged to zero in on the essence of assessment validity by remembering it equals *inference accuracy*. Similarly, school leaders can arrive at the essence of test reliability by referring to the following equation:

$$\textit{Test Reliability} = \textit{Measurement Consistency}$$

That's right, if educators can mentally equate reliability with consistency, they have a pretty solid lock on the meaning of assessment reliability. And, of course, consistency of measurement should definitely be regarded as a *positive* attribute of a test. It should be apparent that if a test is *inconsistently* measuring something, then educators would have to get lucky to come up with an accurate score-based inference about the students who completed the inconsistent test. The more consistency an assessment instrument possesses, the better it is for those who use the assessment instrument.

Three Kinds of Consistency

Just as we saw there are three potential kinds of validity evidence to be used when crafting a validity argument, it is similarly true that there are three kinds of test-consistency evidence that can be assembled when determining a test's consistency. But, because these types of reliability evidence are, unlike validity evidence, focused on a test itself, we usually think of them as three distinctive *types of reliability*. A school leader needs to know what those three sorts of reliability are and, above all, needs to know *that they are not interchangeable*. That's right; the three kinds of test reliability endorsed by the APA-AERA-NCME *Standards* are definitely not the same, as you will soon see. Each of those three sorts of reliability is needed when an educational test is employed in a distinctive way. Let's briefly see what these three kinds of reliability evidence are.

Stability Reliability

If you were to ask most educators to describe the nature of test reliability, they'd usually say something such as, "A test is reliable if a student who takes the test at different times gets pretty similar scores." This is a widespread perception of what's meant by reliability, and it's not wrong. But this conception of test reliability represents *only one* kind of reliability, and it is called *stability reliability* or, sometimes, it is described as *test-retest reliability.* Evidence of a test's stability reliability is especially useful when students are allowed to complete significant tests on different days during any sort of extended "test administration window." In many states, the test-administration window for annual accountability tests often extends over a period of several weeks.

To secure evidence of a test's stability reliability, we administer the test to a group of students, wait for some period of time, then readminister the same test to the same students. What we are looking for is evidence that students' scores on the two testing occasions are similar. The interval between the two test administrations can vary substantially, and it might be only a few hours, or it might be a few months. It is important, of course, that no intervening events (such as test-focused instruction) occur between the two testing occasions that would influence students' scores on the second test administration, for example, giving students intensive between-test instruction dealing with whatever is being tested.

In studying the reliability of two sets of students' scores, two analytic methods are routinely applied these days, but in years past only one way of looking at reliability data was used, that is, a *correlation* analysis. A correlation coefficient is a numerical index, ranging from +1.00 to −1.00, with high positive numbers indicating a strong positive relationship between two sets of scores and negative numbers indicating the opposite. Coefficients around zero reflect little or no relationship between the two sets of variables (that is, in this instance, test scores). To demonstrate that a test has suitable stability reliability, therefore, one hopes to find a strong positive correlation coefficient, that is, *a reliability coefficient* of, say, +.75 or higher, depending on the level of care that was given to the test's development, the length of the interval between the test and retest, and the nature of what is being assessed. (Students' mastery of some educational skills or bodies of knowledge tend to be more constant—between tests—than others.) Correlation-based reliability coefficients have, for many decades, been the way reliability evidence has been reported for almost all educational tests.

In recent years, a second and increasingly popular way of describing a test's reliability has been to report the test's *classification consistency,* that is, the degree to which consistent classifications about test-takers' performances are made in a test-and-retest situation. This approach to describing a test's reliability is also referred to as *decision consistency* because, in many instances, decisions regarding test-takers are linked to the classifications assigned to those test-takers. To illustrate, suppose that a test is being used to classify students into three achievement categories: *basic, proficient,* and *advanced.* Based on which of these three categories a student ends up in, the student will be given different types of instruction. Clearly, then, an instructional decision is linked to the student's test-determined classification. Well, when analyzing students' test-retest data from a decision-consistency perspective, we don't look all that carefully at the student's specific numerical score, but, rather, we consider into which classification this score places the student. To illustrate, suppose we were using a new accountability test that yielded scores ranging from 0 to 80, and the following classifications had been previously determined for categorizing students' scores:

Classification	Test Score
Basic	0–54
Proficient	55–68
Advanced	69–80

To illustrate, if Shauna earned a score of 64 on the first test administration and a score of 55 on the second administration, Shauna would have been classified as *proficient* on both tests even though there was a nine-point difference between her two scores. So, for Shauna, a consistent classification would have been made on the basis of her two substantially different test scores. To determine a test's stability reliability using a classification-consistency approach, all we do is report the percentage of identical-classifications on the two testing occasions. Thus, an 87 percent classification-consistency index for a particular test would indicate that 87 percent of the students had been classified identically based on the two test administrations as seen in the illustrative results below for a test-retest reliability study.

Classification on the Two Test Administrations	Percent of Students in Test-Retest Reliability Study
Basic Both Times	38 percent
Proficient Both Times	40 percent
Advanced Both Times	9 percent
Different Categories	13 percent
Classification-Consistency = 87 percent	

One advantage of the classification-consistency approach is that it tends to be more intuitively understandable to most people, whereas correlation-based reliability coefficients are definitely less so. Another advantage of the classification-consistency approach is that it exemplifies the inherent imprecision of educational assessment, that is, the imprecision highlighted in Chapter 1. Educational tests are useful tools. They are not flawless tools. The use of large categories for reporting students' status reminds us that a student who scores at or near a classification's boundaries might, but for the student's performance on an item or two, have been classified in an adjacent category. In a sense, the more modest precision of classification-consistency reliability analyses better reflects the modest precision of the tests we use to make those classifications.

Wrapping up stability reliability, then, we see it is an approach to reliability determination for a test that calls for the same students to take the same test twice, and those students' scores on the test are then analyzed using traditional correlational approaches and/or classification-consistency approaches. Whichever analytic approach is used, the results are heavily influenced by factors such as (1) the length of the interval between testing, (2) whether any test-relevant occurrences have taken place between the two tests, (3) the quality with which the test was developed, and (4) the nature of what is being assessed. But in situations when a previously absent student might be allowed to take, for instance, an accountability test sometime later during a three-week "makeup window," there is clearly a need for reliability evidence of the stability sort.

Alternate-Form Reliability

A second kind of reliability is nicely described by its name, that is, *alternate-form reliability*. Many instances now exist when, usually for test-security purposes, educators need to employ more than one form of a test. What we are trying to discover via this second approach to reliability is simply how consistent test-takers' scores are on the two forms. As was the case with stability reliability, the same students take two tests, but in this instance both of the tests are different, that is, alternate forms of the same test. To be more precise, *most* of the items on the two forms are different. That's because it is increasingly common to include a subset of identical items on the two forms. These identical items, usually referred to as "anchor items" or "linking items", can be used to make statistical adjustments so, if it turns out that one form of the test is decisively more difficult than the other form, the individuals who analyze the results can engage in some statistical high-jinks to render students' *adjusted* performances on the two test-forms more comparable.

When collecting alternate-form evidence of reliability, the delay between students' taking the two different forms can vary. But because the focus in this instance is on the comparability of the two forms, the delay between administration of the two forms is usually quite short, for instance, a few days.

The data resulting from an alternate-forms type of reliability study are analyzed in the same way that we saw with stability reliability, that is, either by employing a correlation-based reliability coefficient or by using a classification-consistency approach. Given the particulars of the situation, especially with carefully constructed alternate forms, reliability coefficients can reach the high +.80s or the low +.90s, and classification-consistency indices can exceed 90 percent based on the percent of identically classified test-takers.

Internal Consistency Reliability

The third member of our reliability trio is a decisively different sort of creature, not only in the way we collect evidence about it, but in what it really signifies. *Internal consistency reliability*, as with the other two kinds of reliability evidence, is accurately labeled. When we collect evidence about the internal consistency of a test, we are trying to find out how consistently the items in that test function. In other words, we want to discover whether the items on the test are doing the same sort of measurement job, that is, whether they're behaving homogeneously as they measure whatever they're measuring.

To collect internal-consistency reliability evidence, only a single administration of the test is required. Test-takers' performances on the test's individual items are then analyzed so that an estimate is provided of the homogeneity with which the items are measuring a test-taker's performance. The resulting index is akin to a correlation coefficient ranging from −1.00 to +1.00. High positive internal-consistency coefficients indicate that the items on a test are, indeed, doing the same kind of job in measuring whatever the test is measuring. Many nationally standardized achievement tests, because of the considerable care with which they are developed, when analyzed for internal consistency, come up with coefficients as high as +.95.

For calculating a test's internal consistency, among the most common analytic approaches used are the *Kuder-Richardson* procedures, usually referred to as K-R indices. K-R procedures can be employed with items that are scored *dichotomously* (items scored as correct or incorrect). However, when a test's items can be assigned different numbers of points, that is, when scored as a *polytomous* item, *Cronbach's coefficient alpha* is the preferred procedure. What's most important to recall is that when internal-consistency coefficients are positive and high, this indicates a test's items are doing the same measurement job.

What a school leader needs to understand about this third kind of reliability approach is that it is, by far, the most likely to be encountered. After all, to calculate an internal-consistency coefficient requires only one test administration, not two (as is necessary with the other two versions of reliability evidence). But what you also must recognize is that in order for an internal-consistency estimate of reliability to be high, the test's items must be essentially measuring the same thing, namely, a *single* educational variable of some sort. So, an achievement test in mathematics with a high internal-consistency coefficient must contain items that, at least in some sense, measure a general variable such as a student's "mathematical understanding." Similarly, a reading test with a high coefficient alpha will typically contain items focused on measuring a student's "reading comprehension." Note that what must be measured by tests with high, positive internal-consistency estimates are broad grain-size educational variables.

However, strong internal-consistency estimates for achievement tests indicate, unfortunately, that those tests *cannot be instructionally diagnostic* in a way that teachers can obtain an instructionally useful fix on what it is their students can and can't do. Remember, to the extent that an achievement test is trying to measure students' mastery of, say, a half-dozen *different* skills or bodies of knowledge, then the test's internal-consistency estimates are certain to plummet. We have a long history of having our standardized achievement tests measure students' mastery of a single, comprehensive variable. The makers of standardized achievement tests took pride, over the years, in their tests' excellent reliability (of the internal-consistency variety). But the very qualities that contribute to excellent internal consistency turn out to work against supplying teachers with the more fine-grained information they need in order to make instructional decisions regarding students' mastery of different skills and bodies of knowledge. If an achievement test sets out to assess students' mastery of discernibly distinctive curricular aims, it then is impossible for all the test's items to be measuring the same thing. There are, by deliberate design, different things being measured.

As you can probably guess, indicators of a test's internal consistency are reported only as correlation coefficients (such as coefficient alpha or as one of the K-R formulae), not as classification-consistency percentages. After all, there are no two classifications of test-takers occurring, only a focus on the homogeneity of a test's items. Internal-consistency reliability revolves around the consistency of *what's going on inside a test;* the other two kinds of reliability evidence are based on the consistency of *test-takers' performances.*

Internal Consistency and Hobgoblins

In the 19th century, Ralph Waldo Emerson concluded that, "A foolish consistency is the hobgoblin of little minds." One wonders what Emerson might have thought if he'd been obliged to spend much time dealing with educational testing's internal-consistency reliability coefficients.

If we were somehow able to magically collect all the reliability coefficients ever computed for educational tests, then plop those coefficients into three containers representing the three varieties of assessment reliability, by far the heftiest of those containers would need to be the one containing internal-consistency coefficients. This is because the calculation of internal-consistency coefficients is so very much easier than the calculation of either stability coefficients or alternate-form coefficients. So, when most educators bump into a reliability coefficient during their careers, odds are that the bumped coefficient will be some sort of an internal-consistency index.

Nevertheless, there's a definite sense in which "Internal consistency is the hobgoblin of little psychometric minds." Put differently, although a set of wonderful internal-consistency coefficients may make a testing specialist's heart palpitate more rapidly, what good are such coefficients to in-the-trenches teachers? The answer to that "What good?" question is, regrettably, *not much!*

Just think about it for a moment. Most teachers need to know what *specific* skills or *particular* bodies of knowledge their students have or haven't mastered. Teachers want this information before instruction takes place and, most certainly, need it after instruction is finished. Teachers almost always focus their instruction not on some amorphous amalgam of merged-together knowledge and skills but on a medley of more specific skills and bodies of knowledge.

However, for teachers to get a reasonable fix on such skills and knowledge, the tests being used must contain a sufficient number of *different* sorts of items to tease out a student's grasp of the different knowledge and skills being assessed. Yet, to the extent that a test's items are focused on measuring genuinely *different* things, the test's internal-consistency coefficient will shrink. Remember, high internal-consistency coefficients exist when the vast majority of a test's items are *homogeneously* measuring the same thing. But the more general a test's assessment focus is, the less useful that test will be for instructional diagnosis. In other words, when a flock of discrete skills and bodies of knowledge are smashed together under the umbrella of a single, yet fundamentally cryptic variable, the result may yield high internal-consistency indices. But the test will provide little instructionally relevant information to teachers.

Consistency is an oft-lauded commodity. But when it comes to the internal consistency of educational tests, consistency sometimes looks like a hobgoblin.

Profound Differences

Looking at the three kinds of reliability evidence just described, you can see why one of the crucial understandings a school leader must possess regarding test reliability is represented in Figure 3.1 where the three versions of reliability are depicted as being definitely *unequal* to one another.

Although all three kinds of test reliability deal with a test's consistency of measurement, they are focused on decisively different aspects of consistency. Yet, when many educators

Figure 3.1   The Nonequivalence of the Three Types of Evidence Regarding a Test's Reliability

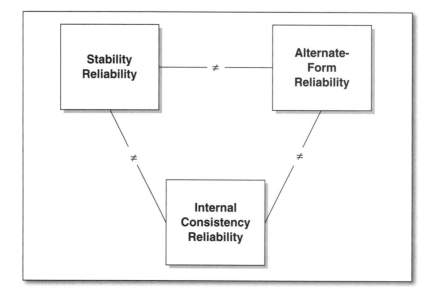

think about the reliability of tests, they do not realize that what's reported as "a test's reliability" may arrive in one of three very different flavors. More often than not, you'll find a test's reliability reported as its internal consistency. This is chiefly because the data needed to compute internal-consistency coefficients are easier to obtain than what's required for the other two kinds of reliability evidence. But merely because a test has a high internal-consistency coefficient, this tells us nothing about the test's stability or the degree to which different forms of that test would yield consistent results. Accordingly, when reviewing a test's suitability, school leaders need to consider whether the kind of consistency evidence being provided appropriately meshes with the intended uses of the test. The three kinds of reliability evidence are fundamentally different.

ASSESSMENT CONSISTENCY
FOR INDIVIDUAL STUDENTS

Although we have seen that the three *Standards*-approved sorts of reliability are focused on very different kinds of consistency, those three reliability types do have one thing in common: They are concerned with the consistency of the test itself rather than with the consistency of an individual's score. It is true, of course, if a test's stability reliability is quite high, then educators can be reasonably sure that if Harold takes a graduation test during April instead of May, Harold's score on the April test is apt to be similar to the score he would have earned had he taken the test in May. *But how similar?*

We turn, now, to an important kind of test consistency that's centered on the consistency of an *individual test-taker's performance*. The indicator that helps us determine the consistency of an individual test-taker's score is called the *standard error of measurement*, often identified by the abbreviation SEM. Please think of a standard error of measurement as a numerical representation of the consistency of an individual's score on the test if that test had been taken by the same student again and again and—for good measure—again and again. Because few students would be willing to take the same test even twice, much less as part of an infinite test-taking regimen, we use an SEM to *estimate* how much variability would be present if a test were, indeed, readministered oodles of times.

An SEM is interpreted in much the same way that opinion pollsters use error margins to reflect the accuracy of sample-based opinions. For instance, when we see a newspaper report that 59 percent of a state's citizens are likely to vote in favor of a particular candidate in an upcoming election, this 59 percent figure is often accompanied by a footnote indicating there is a "plus-or-minus sampling error of 3 percent." A standard error of measurement functions in the same fashion—with smaller SEMs indicating less variability (conversely, more consistency)—associated with a student's test performance. The smaller the sampling error margins on opinion polls, the more confident we can be in the accuracy of the poll's reported numbers. Similarly, the smaller the SEMs for a test, the more confident we can be in the accuracy of a student's test performance.

The size of an SEM is based on two factors: (1) the *variability* of test-takers' scores on the test and (2) the *reliability* of the test. If only a small spread in test-takers' scores is present, and there's also a high reliability coefficient, then there will be a small SEM. Conversely, if there is a large spread among students' scores or if the reliability of the test is low, then there will be a large SEM.

Educators can use SEMs to arrive at a defensible conclusion about the likely accuracy of a student's performance on a particular test. This is accomplished by interpreting the student's score according to the probabilities of scores associated with a normal probability distribution. To illustrate, suppose Sally has earned a score of 48 on a 65-item test and there is an SEM for that test of 3.0. If we add one SEM to Sally's raw score of 48 and subtract one SEM from that 48, we end up with a range of 45 to 51, that is, Sally's 48 plus and minus one SEM of 3.0. Just as in a normal probability distribution, where plus and minus one standard deviation from the mean includes 68 percent of the scores, the range of 45 to 51 tells us that if Sally were to retake the 65-item test an infinite number of times, her score would probabilistically fall within the plus-and-minus one SEM range about 68 percent of the time.

If we were to use two SEMs in this example involving Sally, we'd add two SEMs to her raw score of 48 and subtract two SEMs from the 48 to end up at a range of between 42 and 54. That two-SEM range, both plus and minus, signifies that if Sally retook the same test a huge number of times, then about 95 percent of the time her score would end up within that plus and minus two-SEM range. This is the same as we would see in a normal distribution where, within plus and minus two standard deviations of the mean, we find 95 percent of the distribution.

As you can see, the smaller a test's standard error of measurement is, the more confidence we can have in the accuracy of a student's performance. SEMs supply educators with reasonable ways of estimating how much confidence to place in an individual student's test score. SEMs become particularly important when school leaders confront the implications of making mistakes as they classify students. This is because, good intentions notwithstanding, educators *will make mistakes* in the way they classify test-takers. Educational testing is far too imprecise for educators to always dodge such mess ups. Two kinds of mistakes can be made on the basis of students' test scores—*false positives* or *false negatives*. A student is a *false positive* when judged as being able to do something that, in fact, the student cannot do. For instance, if a student scores above a previously determined cut score on a science test, we conclude that the student can, indeed, perform the scientific skills measured by the test. But what if the student actually can't perform those skills? What if the student just got lucky and, if administered the same test again or given a comparable version of that test, the student would score below the cut score? Conversely, a student might be identified as someone who could *not* perform the scientific skills on the basis of a test, yet the student actually possesses complete mastery of those scientific skills. This second student would be a *false negative*.

In many instances, the consequences of false negatives and false positives are not the same. For example, when trying to decide whether students have mastered a given curricular aim, such as a cognitive skill or a body of knowledge, a false positive is usually more serious than a false negative. False positives indicate that a student has actually mastered the curricular aim when, in fact, the student hasn't. As a consequence, rather than being given additional instruction that the student needs, no further instruction might be supplied to the student. That's often a serious instructional mistake.

A false negative in the same sort of situation would lead to a mistake, but it's a mistake that's more benign. Let's say that George, on the basis of a test whose SEM is quite large, has been falsely identified as not having mastered a particular curricular aim when, in fact, he really has mastered the aim. Accordingly, George is likely to be given additional, but unnecessary, instruction dealing with the curricular aim being assessed. Because it seems far less serious to heap extra instruction on a student who *doesn't* need it than to withhold additional instruction from a student who does need it, most educators would agree that in situations involving the potential need for additional instruction, *unless it happens too often,* a false-negative mistake is less worrying than is a false-positive mistake.

In other contexts, false negatives might be more educationally significant than false positives. What a school leader needs to do when dealing with these sorts of potential assessment-based mistakes is, as always, consider the size of a test's standard error of measurement then decide whether there is any substantial difference in importance between false positives and false negatives. After considering both of these points, it may well be this is one of those occasions when it becomes all too clear that significant educational decisions should not be made on the basis of a student's performance on only one test. The shakier the assessment evidence associated with a decision, the more zealously a school leader should be looking for additional evidence to support or negate the inference-based decision to be made.

RELIABILITY AND VALIDITY: STRANGE BEDFELLOWS?

It is said that, "Politics makes strange bedfellows." Although, to my knowledge, I have never actually met a "bedfellow" or even suspected someone of being "a strange bedfellow," I think I understand that politics sometimes obliges people of different political persuasions to splash in the same wading pool. Well, because validity and reliability are generally conceded to be the meat and potatoes of educational assessment, are these two bedfellows compatible or not?

Here's the quick answer, and it's one that school leaders need to have firmly in mind: *Reliable tests can provide evidence from which valid or invalid score-based inferences can be made, but valid score-based inference cannot be made from unreliable tests.* The preceding italicized words, if said rapidly, can turn into a serious tongue twister; but what they mean is straightforward. Because unreliable tests supply inconsistent results, it is clearly impossible to routinely come up with valid score-based inferences based on those inconsistent results. For a few students, of course, even on an unreliable test, it's possible that a score-based inference will be accurate. Flukes happen.

But a superbly reliable test, even though it simply oozes consistency, might yield scores from which absurdly inaccurate inferences are made. To illustrate, let's say you and some colleagues had developed two forms of a remarkably consistent new test of students' historical knowledge. You have collected all three kinds of reliability evidence—that is, stability, alternate-form, and internal consistency—and for all three variants of reliability, the resulting reliability coefficients ranged between .85 and .95. The new test, as one of your colleagues happily observes, "Simply reeks of reliability!" Yet, suppose you tried to use students' performances on your new history test to predict those students' ability to pole vault. High scorers on the test would be predicted to pole vault well, and low scorers would be predicted to pole vault poorly. (This, of course, would be a remarkably silly use of students' scores on a history test.) What I am attempting to illustrate with this absurd example from an ultrareliable test, is that it's still possible to come up with rotten test-based inferences. Excellent reliability does not guarantee valid test-based inferences. However, valid test-based inferences presume the presence of satisfactory test reliability.

What do educators really need to know about reliability—and what do they need to do with what they know about this concept? Well, just as all health practitioners should understand what's meant by a person's blood pressure, yet may not personally need to measure each person's blood pressure, all educators should have at least a general understanding of the nature of test reliability. But there is little need for teachers to *compute* reliability evidence for their own classroom assessments. Oh, perhaps for one or two super-important classroom exams, a teacher might actually calculate reliability coefficients, but this sort of activity will typically deflect from what teachers truly should be up to—instruction. School leaders, therefore, need not urge classroom teachers to collect reliability evidence—of any sort—for their classroom assessments. On the other hand, as the significance of educational assessments becomes greater, school leaders should definitely have a solid understanding of what's going on when we say, "This test is reliable." This means there are certain understandings related to reliability that are, indeed, crucial.

CRUCIAL UNDERSTANDINGS

Test reliability is an interesting commodity. In this chapter, you saw that there are several varieties of reliability, and they are definitely not the same. Moreover, you saw that we can report at test's reliability as a correlation-based *reliability coefficient* or as a *percent of consistent classifications*. Because we are concerned about the consistency of an individual test-taker's performance, considerable attention should be given to a test's *standard error of measurement* (SEM), with smaller SEMs indicating that a test measures with greater consistency. Finally, we considered the relationship between reliability and validity. Blending all of this reliability information, along with sufficient crushed ice, you end up with a rather delicious "reliability smoothie" revolving around the following three crucial understandings.

CRUCIAL UNDERSTANDINGS

- Test reliability refers to the consistency with which a test measures what it is measuring, but the three professionally accepted types of reliability, that is, stability, alternate-form, and internal consistency, represent fundamentally different ways of looking at a test's measurement consistency.
- A test's reliability is usually reported either as a correlation-based reliability coefficient or as the percentage of test-takers' identical classifications on different test administrations, but because internal-consistency estimates of reliability are based on a single test administration, internal consistency is reported only as a reliability coefficient.
- A test's standard error of measurement, based on the test's variability as well as its reliability, should be employed to determine the consistency of an individual student's test performance—with smaller SEMs indicating more consistent assessment.

RECOMMENDED READING*

American Educational Research Association. (1999). *Standards for educational and psychological testing.* Washington, DC: Author.

Stiggins, R. J. (2008). *An introduction to student-involved assessment for learning* (5th ed.). Upper Saddle River, NJ: Prentice-Hall/Merrill.

Thorndike, R. M., & Thorndike-Christ, T. (2010). *Measurement in psychology and education* (8th ed.). Boston: Pearson.

---

* Complete bibliographic information and brief annotations are supplied for the following recommendations in the Reading Recommendations Roundup (pp. 181–190).

4

Assessment Bias

What school leaders need to know about *assessment bias* can be summed up in the following, multiclause sentence: Assessment bias exists, it is harmful, it is far less prevalent today than it was in the past, and its reduction has been brought about by the use of judgmental and empirical bias-detection techniques. In this chapter, we'll be looking at the nature of assessment bias, why it is so damaging, and how we can eliminate, or at least markedly reduce, bias in our educational tests.

WHAT IS ASSESSMENT BIAS?

Assessment bias refers to the qualities of a test that *offend* or *unfairly penalize* test-takers because of those test-takers' personal qualities such as their gender, race, ethnicity, religion, or similar group-defining characteristics. In truth, if we were to ask most educators, "What do people mean when they say a test is biased?" we'd usually get accurate responses from most people. Educators surely understand that biased tests don't give certain groups of students a fair chance to succeed and, therefore, assessment bias is a decidedly undesirable attribute in a test. But a school leader needs to know more. A school leader needs to understand just where assessment bias comes from. As you saw in the opening sentence of this paragraph, assessment bias can be caused by two culprits, namely, the *offensiveness* of a test item or an item's *unfair penalization* of certain test-takers. Let's look more carefully at each of those two sources of assessment bias.

Offensiveness

Assessment bias is present in an educational test when one or more of its items *offend* (that is, irritate, annoy, or anger) certain students because those students happen to be members of a particular group. For instance, if a test item implies that females are incapable of attaining high political office, this item would (and should) offend any girls taking the test in which the offending item appears. When an item offends a student, the student's performance on subsequent items is apt to be adversely affected. If, for instance, an offensive item were encountered by a student halfway through a test, odds are that the student's performance on the second half of the test might be less successful than the student's performance on the test's first half. Students who are irritated, annoyed, or angry rarely perform as well as do students who are swathed in serenity.

To help you think about the issue of offensiveness for a moment, please mentally slip inside the skin of a person who belongs to a group that has just been blatantly insulted by a test item. Think about how you—personally—would be likely to respond. Suppose, for example, you are a conservative Christian, and that an early item on a test clearly mocks conservative Christians by referring to them as "Unthinking Bible Thumpers." Having been sufficiently incensed by the item writer's insensitivity—if not outright enmity toward Christians—can you see how your reaction to subsequent items on the test might be affected? At the very least, you are apt to be somewhat distracted by the offensive item. And if that distraction becomes intense, you might end up answering incorrectly a number of items that, without the distraction, you would have answered correctly.

Other instances of offensive content in test items can be seen whenever slurs slide into items based on stereotypic negatives about members of particular ethnic groups (for example, Mexican or Puerto Rican Latinos) or racial groups (for example, African Americans or Asian Americans). As you will see later in the chapter, considerable attention has been given in recent years by measurement specialists to the identification and elimination of such biased content, but occasionally some slurs still slither into items.

To illustrate an instance of assessment bias flowing from the offensiveness of an item, please consider the social studies item seen in Figure 4.1. I constructed this item only to illustrate how an unthinking item developer can create an item genuinely offensive to certain groups of students. In Figure 4.1's fictional item, you will see the correct answer is Choice C, but that the other three answer choices are all quite demeaning to students who were born in Mexico or who have family members who were born in Mexico. If you were a sixth grader

Figure 4.1   A Sixth-Grade Social Studies Item Likely to Offend a Particular Subgroup of Students

Which one of the following statements best describes a current immigration reality in the southwestern United States?

   A. Given Mexico's inability to control its own drug gangs, Mexican immigrants are less welcome in the United States than are immigrants from elsewhere.

   B. Immigrants from Mexico, whether legal or illegal, have rarely ended up being economically successful in the United States.

  *C. Public opinion among U.S. citizens varies substantially about how best to deal with the nation's immigration issues.

   D. Because of Mexican immigrants' inability to speak English properly, most of those immigrants are destined to hold menial jobs in the United States.

answering this item, and your parents came to the United States from Mexico, how do you think you would feel about the gratuitous discounting of Mexico in Choices A, B, and D? I admit that Figure 4.1's illustrative item is "over the top" when it comes to offensiveness, but items containing similarly reprehensible content occasionally appear even on significant educational assessments.

Sometimes assessment bias will not be found in individual items, but may bubble up in the complete array of a test's items. For instance, suppose in a 60-item mathematics word-problem test there were 15 items scattered throughout the test involving Native Americans. In essentially all of those 15 items, the fictitiously depicted Native American was always portrayed as working in a low-level, poorly paid position. Although not one of these items, in and of itself, might be regarded as offensive, the collectivity of the items would be seen by many Native American test-takers as subtly but certainly offensive. As soon as this pattern of multi-item offensiveness had been sensed by any Native American test-taker, that student's performance on subsequent items is apt to be lower than it otherwise would have been.

What we see, then, is that offensiveness of a test item reduces the quality of a test-taker's performance on that item and on later items. As such, assessment bias leads to lessened accuracy in a student's score on the total test by lowering what that performance might have been had no offensive-based bias been present.

Unfair Penalization

A second source of assessment bias, and one that's often more difficult to identify, occurs when one or more items in an educational test *unfairly penalizes* a student based on that student's personal characteristics. Unfair penalization is tougher to spot because it often lurks subtly in an item rather than leaping out as an easily detectible slur against particular groups.

It is important, however, for this kind of penalization to be genuinely *unfair*, and not simply to distinguish between students who study properly and students who don't. Suppose, for example, a rarely serious student invariably goofs off instead of studying diligently. Suppose further, as a predictable result of such off-goofing, the student answers an item incorrectly and is, therefore, penalized for this mistaken response. The resultant wrong-answer penalty is consummately *fair*, not *unfair*. Merely because items are missed does not land those items in the unfair-penalization pile. What's required for assessment bias to be present is for the penalization to *unfairly* flow from a student's personal characteristics.

Here's a fictitious example of how a test items on a mathematics test might be biased against female test-takers. Please imagine that this make-believe math test was created by Mr. Rodney, a serious sports fan who teaches general mathematics to ninth graders. Mr. Rodney peppers his tests with word problems because he thinks such problems allow him to make more valid inferences about whether his students can apply in-school mathematics to real-world problems. However, because Mr. Rodney's out-of-school life revolves almost totally around sports, particularly professional basketball, baseball, and football, he creates sports-related items for almost all of his word-problem tests. After all, the world of sports is where his thoughts typically are, and professional sports happen to be laden with a galaxy of nifty numerical operations.

Unfortunately, as he constructs his items, Mr. Rodney sometimes employs abbreviations likely to be known only to those who are also sports fans. For example, his baseball-based items sometimes, with scant amplification, refer to RBIs (that is, "runs batted in"), his football problems include numbers based on YAC (that is, "yards gained after a catch"), and in basketball he often refers to "trifectas" (that is, baskets made from behind the three-point line). In general, more boys follow these professional sports than do girls. So, as a consequence, a meaningfully greater proportion of girls than boys end up having trouble with Mr. Rodney's sports-related items. Although some boys don't possess the sports lingo that frequently finds its way into Mr. Rodney's word problems, a greater percent of girls are baffled by the tests' sometimes cryptic sports terms and abbreviations. Accordingly, the female students in Mr. Rodney's math classes tend to score lower on his tests than do his male students. The girls' scores, therefore, often underestimate what those girls actually know about the mathematics being taught by Mr. Rodney. Whether he knows it or not, his tests unfairly penalize his female students.

In many of our most important, professionally developed tests, there's an insidious, unfair penalization of certain student groups, and it stems from a student's socioeconomic status (SES), that is, the level of affluence of a student's family. We'll see more about the harmful impact of SES-based items in the next chapter, but you'll find a substantial number of such items even in high-stakes tests. These sorts of SES-linked items give an edge to students coming from more affluent backgrounds. Certain subtleties in an item's content or phrasing, often not recognized by the individual who originally created the test item, can make the item more likely to be answered correctly by students from higher-SES backgrounds than by their less-affluent classmates.

Okay, in addition to possible offensiveness, you've now seen that a second contributor to assessment bias in a particular test item is that the item unfairly penalizes a particular group of test-takers on the basis of that group's personal characteristics. A given item can be biased on the basis of either of these factors or, if the item is particularly poor, it can be both offensive and can also unfairly penalize certain groups of test-takers.

WHY IS ASSESSMENT BIAS SO REPREHENSIBLE?

Tests are built by human beings, and human beings make mistakes. So, it is certainly not surprising that some items on any educational assessment will turn out to be less than wonderful. But why is it that assessment bias seems to receive so much attention these days? Indeed, why is assessment bias so terrible? The answer to those questions, put simply, is that *assessment bias vitiates assessment validity.* Recalling that the major measurement mission of an educational test is to provide educators with the evidence they need to arrive at valid inferences about students' covert status, assessment bias clearly mucks up the validity of those score-based inferences.

Because of the offensiveness and/or unfair penalization of a test's items, when certain groups of students score less well than they otherwise would have scored, we will almost certainly arrive at invalid inferences about how well those students have mastered whatever is being assessed. We will, based on a flawed interpretation of a test's results, conclude that certain students have not mastered particular skills or bodies of knowledge when, in fact, they most certainly have. We may end up, then, frequently providing those students with totally redundant instruction focused on already mastered curricular aims. Those students will be educationally short-changed because they aren't permitted to pursue additional curricular aims—having been mired in trying to learn things they have already learned. A waste.

Don't You Dare!

Almost 20 years ago, I directed a test-development organization that created high-stakes tests for about a dozen states. Our very first state-level test-development project was in South Carolina where we were commissioned to create a series of high-stakes accountability tests to be called the South Carolina Basic Skills Assessment Program (BSAP). One of the important tasks during such a test-development effort is to make sure a test's items are not biased against any group of test-takers.

So, early on in the test-development process, we established a BSAP Bias Review Committee composed of about 30 experienced South Carolina educators, roughly half of whom were African American teachers. As soon as a sufficient numbers of items had been generated, we called in the committee whose members evaluated the items, one-by-one, to see if the items were apt to offend or unfairly penalize any group of South Carolina students. Based on this initial review, a number of potentially biased items were sent scurrying to the shredder.

(Continued)

(Continued)

But then, a few months later, we carried out a large-scale field test of the surviving items with several thousand South Carolina students. Students' responses to the potential BSAP items were analyzed so that we could see whether there were any meaningful differences in the performance of the state's white students and African American students. Again, we called together the BSAP Bias Review Committee to guide us regarding which items, based on the field-test data, might be jettisoned.

I moderated the meeting and, because it was the first one of its kind I had ever attended, I regarded the upcoming meeting with more than a dollop of apprehension. I was apprehensive chiefly because results of the field test revealed that about a quarter of the field-tested items had been answered correctly far less often by African American students than by their white classmates. I anticipated that the Bias Review Committee would insist we reject any items that had been missed far more frequently by African American students than by white students. But my apprehensiveness was unwarranted.

Although a small number of the prospective BSAP items did, in fact, bite the dust because of defects revealed by the field test, when it came to the items missed more often by African American students, it was the African American members of the Bias Review Committee who urged us to retain the items. More than one of those educators said to me, in essence, "Don't you dare remove the items! Those items measure important things that *all* of our state's students—including our African American students—need to learn. If you delete those items from the test, we'll not know what we need to be working on instructionally. Our state's African American youngsters simply haven't been taught well enough so far. We need to teach them better so they can answer these kinds of items correctly!"

And so it was that I learned an important lesson. A test item for which there is a disparate impact on different groups of test-takers may not, merely because of its disparate impact, be biased. The BSAP bias reviewers saw no assessment bias in almost all of the items on which there was a disparate impact between white and African American students. What the bias reviewers concluded, instead, was that there were prior instructional inadequacies adversely affecting the performance of those African American youngsters. Committee members wanted those inadequacies addressed instructionally, and so they insisted we retain the deficit-revealing items in the BSAP tests. The bias reviewers were wise.

But beyond the obvious instructionally relevant inaccuracies flowing from biased assessments, there's another significant negative consequence of biased assessments—and it relates to students' *affect*. Biased assessments are, by definition, *unfair*, that is, they are unfair to certain groups of students. Students can be educationally scarred by unfair treatment in school—and this is precisely what's going on when students are asked to complete tests containing items that offend or unfairly penalize those students because, for example, they are Native Americans, African Americans, or because they happen to come from low-SES backgrounds. Unfairly treated kids will typically (and understandably) develop an antipathy toward the source of such unfairness—in this instance, an antipathy toward *school*. The resulting negative affective dispositions can have a long-lasting and harmful impact on how students approach any sort of school-dispensed instruction.

In Chapter 9, we will consider how to go about measuring the affective disposition of student *groups* (not, as you'll see in that chapter, the affective status of *individual* students). However, common sense alone should tell us that if students encounter many biased tests while they're going through school, such experiences can have a long-lasting, negative impact on the way those students react to schooling.

REDUCING ASSESSMENT BIAS

Head back, historically, for a few decades, and you'll discover that the concept of assessment bias rarely, if ever, was discussed during meetings of those who built, scored, and administered our nation's major exams. If assessment bias was ever considered at all, it was given little more than token attention.

I recall vividly a bias-related incident during a graduate course in educational measurement I was teaching at UCLA during the late 70s. I had distributed to my students a set of complimentary materials dealing with one of the nation's nationally standardized achievement tests. Back then, it was thought that such "acts of good will" on the part of a test publisher would generate positive responses subsequently from those students who were preparing to assume leadership positions in the nation's schools. So I was able to order, at no charge, complete sets of tests, technical manuals, and interpretation tables for each of my students. I divided my students into subgroups who studied particular aspects of this widely used standardized test, then reported to the rest of the class on what they had discovered. It seemed to be a useful activity.

Well, on one occasion a subgroup of students had decided to consider the screening procedures the test's publishers had employed in order to eliminate what we had begun to refer to back then as "test bias." When the "test bias" group gave their end-of-course report, they were aghast to tell us that each of the test's potential items had been "reviewed for bias," one item at a time. This bias review had been carried out, individually, by three members of the test firm's staff, two of whom were members of minority groups. Any item that had been identified as biased *by all three reviewers,* was deleted from the pool of eligible items. My students were appropriately outraged at what they regarded as an altogether superficial and staggeringly lenient way of trying to eliminate biased test items.

But then, as the 1980s arrived, we increasingly began to link important decisions to students' scores on significant exams. We began, for example, to deny high school diplomas to low-scoring students on numerous state-installed "minimum competency exams." Indeed, when high-stakes testing became fashionable in American education during the 80s, the potential adverse impact of assessment bias in those high-stakes tests expanded almost exponentially. Assessment specialists realized that they had to get cracking to reduce what was being increasingly recognized as a serious shortcoming in many of the nation's most important educational tests. And, to the credit of the measurement community, get cracking they did.

In passing, you may have noticed that I typically refer to the *reduction* of assessment bias rather than to its *elimination*. This is deliberate. Although the goal of those who focus on assessment bias may be to eradicate it totally from educational tests, bias is a subtle and elusive quarry. Sometimes, simply because we cannot foresee how students will react to a test's items, an item will slip through that—despite our diligent scrutiny—offends or unfairly penalizes certain subgroups of students. So, the aspiration of most test developers will usually not be to expunge assessment bias completely, but a more realistic goal will be to reduce assessment bias in an educational test to an acceptable level—a level where its validity-confounding impact will be minimal.

During the last several decades, two strategies have been employed to reduce assessment bias in important educational tests, a *judgmental strategy* and an *empirical strategy*. As these two approaches are still very much in use today when dealing with the reduction of assessment bias, all school leaders need to understand the essential features of each strategy. Because a judgmentally based approach to the reduction of assessment bias was employed first, we will initially consider that bias-detection strategy.

Judgmental Bias-Detection Strategies

The first, and most obvious, way to tell if a test item might be biased against particular groups of students is simply to look at the item. And this is the essence of what goes on in a judgmental bias-detection strategy. As assessment specialists recognized the need to reduce potential assessment bias in their under-development tests, what they did was appoint a group of reviewers, often experienced teachers, including representatives of the groups most likely to be adversely impacted by the presence of biased test items. For example, if a high-stakes test were being developed for a state whose schools served large numbers of Hispanic American students and a smaller, but meaningful, proportion of African American students, then the reviewers would most certainly include a number of Hispanic American and African American reviewers. This review group, usually referred to as a "Bias-Review Committee" or some similar title, then goes through the not-yet-official items, one-by-one, with each committee member registering an individual judgment regarding the likelihood that each test item is biased. After all of these bias reviewers have made their individual judgments about each item, those judgments are tabulated so that decisions can be made about which test items might be jettisoned.

Typically, bias reviewers are given an orientation to prepare them for their upcoming review tasks then directed to review each item in a pool of items potentially destined for use in a significant educational test. An example of the kind of question those reviewers might face in rendering their per-item judgments is given below.

An Illustrative Question Posed to Bias Reviewers

Might this item offend or unfairly penalize any group of students on the basis of personal characteristics such as gender, ethnicity, religion, or race?

Generally speaking, judgmental bias-review procedures do an excellent job of identifying potentially biased items. Through the use of these sorts of bias-review committees during recent decades, we have dramatically reduced the number of biased items making their way onto important tests. However, at numerous points in a judgmental bias-review process, procedural choices can be made that are apt to render the review process more or less rigorous. School leaders need to recognize that not all judgmental bias-reviews are created equal, and it would be naive for a school leader to assume that merely because a judgmental review of a pool of potential items has been carried out, all items emerging from that review are bias-free.

Let me identify a few of the choice points in the review process that can alter how rigorous a judgmental bias review actually is. For openers, there is the orientation that the review group initially receives. To what degree are the reviewers urged to be demanding or, in contrast, told to be lenient? Then there's the review question itself, a particularly important feature of such reviews. Please look back for a moment at the illustrative question posed above. What would happen if we change the very first word *might,* to the word *will?* I hope you can see that when the question commences with *will, fewer* items will be identified as potentially biased by reviewers than if the question is stated in its current form. When we say *might,* we are asking reviewer to regard an item as potentially biased if there is even a chance that the item *might possibly* offend or unfairly penalize. When the reviewer gets a question starting with *will,* the reviewer needs to be sure that the item *will,* indeed, offend or unfairly penalize students. Slight alterations in the way a reviewer is asked to scrutinize items can make a whopping difference in the number of item-bias judgments supplied by a bias-review committee.

In addition, there is the composition of the Bias-Review Committee itself. Some review committees are composed *exclusively* of minority group members; other committees might have more tokenistic participation by minorities. Another choice point revolves around how many adverse judgments by committee members it takes to eliminate an item. Clearly, those decisions will influence how strictly a review group carries out its task.

What you must recognize is that although the judgmental review of a set of under-development items can be remarkably useful in diminishing assessment bias, the potential for variety in the procedures employed to conduct these reviews is considerable. School leaders dare not assume that all judgmental bias-detection reviews are equivalent. Thus, if you are a school leader who is seriously concerned about the quality of the judgmental bias-detection review associated with a test you are planning to use, there is no substitute for securing the report describing the specifics of the bias-review process. (Such bias-review reports are available, typically from the test's developers, for essentially all high-stakes educational exams.)

Empirical Bias-Detection Strategies

In addition to attempting to reduce assessment bias by judgmentally identifying potentially biased items, the measurement community has also made substantial strides in the use of *empirical approaches* to identify potentially biased items. As soon as test developers began to routinely require all under-development test items to be evaluated by a bias-review panel, most of those test developers also initiated empirical bias-detection techniques. Once there were a sufficient number of items, those items were field tested with fairly large samples of the students for whom the items were ultimately to be used. Based on those field tests, simple comparisons were typically made between the performances of, for example, majority students and any sizable minority groups. In the early days, these analyses were organized around an item's p-value, that is, the proportion of students who answered the item correctly. (For instance, an item answered correctly by 68 percent of test-takers would have a p-value of .68.) So, for example, in a state whose schools were attended by substantial numbers of African American students, the average p-values on each item would be computed for both white and African American field-tested students. Any item where there was a substantial difference between those two average p-values would be subjected to further judgmental scrutiny in an effort to see if the item seemed to be biased.

To illustrate, suppose that on the field test the mean p-value for African American students was .73, but that the mean p-value for white field-test students was .77. Such minor differences are typically disregarded. However, if there were substantial per-item differences between majority test-takers and any group of minority test-takers, for example, a p-value difference of, say, .20 or more, then that item would be seriously reappraised to see if it contained potentially biased elements.

If, for instance, the mean p-value of Hispanic American field-test students on a particular item was .46, while the mean p-value of that same item for white students was .74, then a p-value difference of .28 would cause the item to be reconsidered carefully. Items that, based on their field-test performance, seemed to be biased were typically not used on an operational form of a test, that is, on the test form that really "counted."

During those early contrasts between the field-test performances of different student groups, it became clear that a mere disparity in the performance of different groups of students did not, all by itself, necessarily indicate that assessment bias was present in an item. Disparities in students' performances on an item might, of course, flow exclusively from bias in the item. On the other hand, the lower performance of a group of minority field-tested students could simply reveal that those students had been inadequately instructed. The p-value discrepancies might be attributable to *prior instructional inadequacies* rather than to any bias in a test item. This is a particularly important point for school leaders to recognize, namely, that substantial differences between the performances of minority and majority test-takers may be *either* a function of assessment bias *or* prior instructional disparities. To simply preclude a field-tested item from an operational test because minority field-tested students performed poorly on the item is often shortsighted. It may well be that the minority students did badly on the item because they had not been properly taught what the item was assessing. It is often crucial to retain such items in important exams so that the minority students' inadequate performances can be identified, monitored, and addressed instructionally.

But p-value contrasts between minority and majority groups have long since been replaced by a much more sophisticated procedure known as *differential item functioning* (DIF). DIF analyses, based on all sorts of meaningful computer machinations, do a far more incisive job of letting us know whether a given test item appears to function differently for one group of test-takers than for another. DIF analysis can, because of its computer-based use of all students' test responses to all of a test's items, let us know more precisely whether a given item seems to evoke markedly different responses from different groups of students. Although there are surely subtle variations in the way that DIF analyses are carried out, the underlying premise of such analyses is the same as that employed years earlier when p-value contrasts were first introduced, that is, do different groups of students perform differently on an item?

But, even with DIF analyses of field-test data or, indeed, DIF analyses of real test data, the quandary still exists of whether group differences should be attributed to bias-based deficits in an item or to the caliber of instruction previously received by different groups of students. Although, typically, items for important educational tests are first field tested before being assigned to operational forms of a test, even after items have been included on an actual test, DIF analyses are routinely computed on all items in a test. As a consequence, biased items that might have eluded earlier bias-detection efforts can be identified. Whereas, in years past, we paid little heed to the possibility that assessment bias existed in our tests, now we routinely use a potent blend of judgmental and empirical bias-detection methods to reduce the bias in any high-stakes educational test.

Before wrapping up the chapter with an identification of two crucial understandings related to assessment bias, I wish to raise one issue for consideration by school leaders, and it relates to the level of assessment bias likely to be lurking in teacher-made classroom tests. For those school leaders who work with classroom teachers, please consider bringing to the attention of those teachers the possibility that their teacher-made tests might be biased. A simple explanation of what the two chief contaminants of test items are (that is, offensiveness and unfair penalization) could be followed by an easy-to-follow recommendation that teachers routinely review their tests in an effort to spot, then expunge, possible bias in those tests' items. Many teachers are simply oblivious of the possibility that, inadvertently, their tests may possess biased items. Attentiveness to the chance that assessment bias may be present in teacher-made tests will usually go a long way in diminishing such bias. Teachers just need to be alerted, then given some simple guidelines (such as how to enlist the item-review assistance of minority colleagues) to address this sometimes-serious shortcoming of many classroom tests.

CRUCIAL UNDERSTANDINGS

What's most important for school leaders to understand about assessment bias is that it is harmful, that there are ways of addressing it, and that those ways should be routinely used for any important educational test. Of most significance for school leaders is *a realization that assessment bias may be present in any educational test.* Once this realization is in place, the following crucial understandings can influence a school leader's actions.

CRUCIAL UNDERSTANDINGS

- Assessment bias, the qualities of a test that offend or unfairly penalize test-takers because of group-defining personal characteristics, can seriously diminish the validity of assessment-based inferences about the individuals being offended or unfairly penalized.
- Because two strategies have been employed to identify potentially biased items in educational tests, namely, judgmental and empirical bias-detection strategies, all educators should be familiar with the general nature of each strategy.

RECOMMENDED READING*

McMillan, J. H. (2008). *Assessment essentials for standards-based education* (2nd ed.). Thousand Oaks, CA: Corwin.

Popham, W. J. (2011). *Classroom assessment: What teachers need to know* (6th ed.). Boston: Pearson.

---

* Complete bibliographic information and brief annotations are supplied for the following recommendations in the Reading Recommendations Roundup (pp. 181–190).

Linn, R. L., Miller, D., & Gronlund, N. E. (2008). *Measurement and assessment in teaching* (10th ed.). Upper Saddle River, NJ: Prentice-Hall/Merrill.

Thorndike, R. M., & Thorndike-Christ, T. (2010). *Measurement in psychology and education* (8th ed.). Boston: Pearson.

5

Instructional Sensitivity

If a close friend had recently become a school principal or a superintendent of schools, I'd instantly send my friend a gratis copy of this book. (Don't be impressed by the gratis aspect of this act—authors get pretty hefty discounts.) But I'd probably attach a note saying something such as, "School leaders need to know all of this stuff. However, if you have time for only *one* chapter, make sure to read Chapter 5 about instructional sensitivity. It may save your job."

Let me explain why I think what's in this chapter is so significant. Currently, school leaders are evaluated primarily on the basis of how well their students score on educational accountability tests. There are surely other factors in the evaluative mix when school leaders are appraised, but the level of students' performances on each year's accountability tests is currently the most important determiner of how successful a school leader is thought to be.

To illustrate, let's consider Hypothetical School X (good old HSX). If HSX students' scores on an annual state-administered accountability test are high, then the principal of HSX will be thought to have done an excellent instructional job.

Conversely, and there are numerous "conversely" schools out there these days, when students in Hypothetical School Y (HSY) come up with low scores on the same accountability test, the HSY principal will be regarded by most people, especially by parents of HSY students, as instructionally inept. In short, high test scores are thought to equal effective school leadership; low test scores are thought to equal ineffective school leadership. But, as you'll see in this chapter, those sorts of test-based evaluations of instructional quality, *depending on the tests being used,* can be flat-out wrong. In the chapter's remaining pages, you'll learn why.

School leaders, however, need more than a casual understanding of why it is that some accountability tests provide a misleading indication of instructional quality. For their own professional survival, school leaders must understand this issue *so thoroughly* that they can explain it coherently to the parents and policymakers to whom they, as school leaders, must answer. This chapter will give you the information necessary to explain to a district school-board member, a concerned parent, or a curious citizen why it is that some accountability tests provide an inaccurate picture of instructional quality.

The reason it is particularly important for today's school leaders to understand why certain accountability tests might provide a distorted picture of instructional effectiveness is that, sadly, *most of the accountability tests currently being used to evaluate instructional quality are incapable of doing so.* Thus, if *your* effectiveness as a school leader is going to be judged on the basis of students' scores on an accountability test, and this accountability test is not supplying accurate evidence about instructional quality, then you need to be able to explain to key constituents, including the public at large, why this is so.

Different Quests for Different Tests

In the world of testing, one often runs into classic true-false items. So, to get our consideration of this topic under way, here's such a true-false item for you to answer. Is the following sentence true or false? *"A test is a test is a test is a test."* Well, although the italicized sentence has some serious redundancy problems, what it implies is most definitely *false*. Tests differ, often dramatically, in what they set out to assess. Tests differ, often dramatically, in the kinds of evidence they yield. Tests differ, often dramatically, in how well they can evaluate instructional quality. To regard all tests as equivalent is simply nonsensical. Yet, most citizens and, distressingly, most educators believe all accountability tests are "achievement" tests and all "achievement tests" are essentially interchangeable. This belief is untrue.

A Comparative Lineage

To help you understand how this confused view of education's achievement tests arose, let's take a lightning-fast leap backward into the history of achievement testing in the United States. A good place to start is with the *Army Alpha* of World War I. (That's World War *One*, not World War *Two*.) The *Army Alpha* was a group-administered intelligence test that, during World War I, was administered to nearly 2,000,000 men in an effort to identify U.S. Army recruits who were likely to make good officers. The measurement mission of the *Alpha* was most definitely a *comparative* one. By comparing examinees according to their verbal and quantitative performances, the *Alpha* helped identify the recruits most likely to succeed in officer-training programs. The comparisons among recruits were made by seeing how each test-taker's performance compared to the performances of a previous group of test-takers known as the "norm group." Each recruit's score was assigned a percentile indicating the percent of recruits in the norm group that the recruit's score had exceeded. To illustrate, a recruit whose *Alpha* score was equivalent to a 64th percentile would have outperformed 64 percent of the norm group's test-takers. Recruits who earned high percentiles, for instance, percentiles around 95 or so, were typically sent to officer-training programs. And, by and large, those recruits made good officers. Army officials were genuinely pleased with how well the *Alpha* did its sorting job.

Shortly after World War I, several different testing organizations began to publish "achievement" tests, which—largely because of the success of the *Army Alpha*—were also intended to supply comparative score interpretations about test-takers. To illustrate, the initial version of the *Stanford Achievement Tests,* currently in its 10th version, and one of the nation's most widely used achievement tests, was first published in 1923, only a few years after World War I. The purpose of all those early achievement tests was, like the *Alpha* before them, to *compare* test-takers, that is, to provide scores which allowed those students taking the exams to be compared with each other according to the levels of knowledge and skills possessed. We have continued to rely on this comparative-measurement strategy through the years in our use of nationally standardized achievement tests.

But please note that the comparative strategy embodied in these standardized achievement exams tells us (typically in a given content area, such as mathematics or reading) how test-takers can be compared with respect to the knowledge and skills they possess. Stated differently, standardized achievement tests help us determine, *comparatively,* what students know and can do. Note, however, that these comparative assessments of students' knowledge and skills are not specifically intended to measure *how well those students have been taught.* And, therein, smolders the confusion that has had such an adverse evaluative impact on many schools. A so-called achievement test, intended to measure what students know and can do, is *not* the same thing as a so-called accountability test, intended to measure how well students have been taught.

Different Purposes, Different Score-Based Inferences

If you recall from Chapter 2's treatment of validity, educational assessment is fundamentally a process whereby test-elicited evidence is used in order to make inferences. Well, keeping in mind the overarching importance of test-based inference making, please consider the crucial difference between the following two inferences:

- *Achievement Test Inference:* Test-takers' scores allow us to tell what knowledge and skills those students possess.
- *Accountability Test Inference:* Test-taker's scores allow us to tell how well those students have been taught what the test measures.

As you can see, although many educators might loosely think all accountability tests are achievement tests, and all achievement tests measure students in pretty much the same way, the inferences that can be validly made from achievement tests and from accountability tests are quite different. Most accountability tests, in some general sense, are "achievement" tests. But not all achievement tests have been built so they will accurately measure the effectiveness with which students have been taught.

We have, in the United States, a prevalent measurement belief that students' scores on any test labeled an achievement exam can provide us with an accurate estimate of how well those students have been instructed. This measurement belief is meaningfully mistaken. Most of today's accountability tests have been built in an effort to provide a comparative picture of what students' know and can do, not how well those students have been taught. Most of today's accountability tests, therefore, are apt to provide us with an inaccurate estimate of how well a group of students has been taught.

MISTAKEN EVALUATIONS OF SCHOOLING

Here, in a nutshell, is what happens when the tests we employ to evaluate instructional quality are unable to do so. Because mistakes are made in judging whether instruction is effective, much good instruction will be abandoned and much poor instruction will be allowed to persist.

To illustrate, suppose an inner-city school's teachers have installed a first-rate instructional program during the current school year, and they have assembled a variety of anecdotal and informal assessment evidence to show their instruction is really working well. Students are learning, and students' attitudes toward schooling are getting better and better. The school's new instructional program seems to be humming, purring, and making a host of other success-signifying sounds.

But when the end-of-year accountability test scores are released, it turns out that the school's students don't do well at all on those high-stakes tests. A directive comes careening down from the district superintendent's office to "Modify what you are doing instructionally because evidence from the accountability tests indicates that whatever you are doing instructionally is simply not working." The school's staff will be forced to abandon what may well be a sound instructional program because of the wrong test-based evidence.

On the flip side of the same coin, think about a suburban school that serves students who come chiefly from affluent families. Let's suppose some really rancid instruction is going on in this fictional school, chiefly attributable to the teaching staff's self-satisfied, sometimes lazy approach to their instructional tasks. Put simply, the school is plagued with indifferent and largely ineffectual instruction. Yet, when the state's annual accountability-test scores are published in the local papers, *because of the school's students,* this smug suburban school shines—big time. Those students' high scores on the annual accountability test send a loud, albeit mistaken, signal to the world that the school is doing a great instructional job. So, sadly, the school's inadequate instruction is not likely to be identified. Cruddy, but camouflaged teaching will continue.

The reason these two kinds of mistaken evaluative judgments about instructional quality take place is really quite straightforward. Most accountability tests measure what students bring to school, not what they learn once they arrive.

Two common kinds of accountability tests end up doing an altogether inadequate job of measuring instructional quality.

Traditional Standardized Achievement Tests

One category of unsound accountability test includes nationally standardized accountability tests, such as the *Iowa Tests of Basic Skills* and the *California Achievement Tests*, or even state-built tests constructed along the same traditional lines. The original measurement mission of these traditional tests— assessment instruments we have been using for well over a half-century—was a *comparative* one. It still is. But to accomplish this comparative mission successfully, these tests need to produce a healthy amount of *score spread*, that is, substantial variety in students' total-test scores. What's needed, in order to permit the fine-grained comparisons that are at the very heart of this approach to assessment, are a meaningful number of high scores, a meaningful number of low scores, and lots and lots of middle scores. Indeed, if scores are too bunched up, with a resultant reduction in score spread, then accurate comparisons among test-takers are difficult, if not impossible.

Because most standardized achievement tests must be administered in only about an hour or so (to avoid students' becoming fatigued), it is imperative that many of the test's items contribute appropriately to the needed score spread. After all, a test item that too many students answer correctly, or a test item that too many students answer incorrectly, will not contribute to a sufficient variety in students' total scores. So, what we find in most standardized achievement tests is that a number of items are used in which students' performances are linked either to their parents' socioeconomic status (SES) or to students' inherited academic aptitudes. (You'll see examples of such items later in the chapter.) But while these sorts of items do a terrific job in producing score spread, they usually measure what students bring to school rather than what's learned there.

Thus, accountability tests that adhere to the comparative-measurement mission of traditional standardized achievement testing usually do a dismal job of distinguishing between well taught and poorly taught students. This is true even for an accountability test consisting of a nationally standardized achievement test that has been "augmented" with additional items more closely attuned to a particular state's curricular emphases. This is true even for a built-from-scratch accountability test that adheres to a comparative-measurement strategy in which score spread trumps almost everything else.

Customized Accountability Tests

A second category of accountability test that fails to provide accurate evidence of instructional quality consists of those custom-built tests intended to more accurately reflect the curricular aims (that is, content standards) of a given state or province. These "standards-based" accountability tests, however, soon become dysfunctional in any setting where there are too many content standards to properly assess each year. As a result of teachers' trying to guess *which* content standards will be assessed on an upcoming accountability test, and often guessing wrongly, many of a state's teachers stop giving serious instructional attention to the curricular aims eligible for assessment on a given year's accountability test. The result of teachers' inattention to a state's official curricular aims is that students' test scores are, in time, influenced by the very same factors so potent when standardized achievement tests are used as accountability exams. That's right—students' test scores will be substantially influenced by students' SES and their inherited academic aptitudes. Custom-built standards-based accountability tests, when used in any setting where there are too many curricular targets or insufficient clarity about those targets, will also end up measuring what students bring to school instead of what students are taught there.

Both of these widely used kind of accountability tests—
that is, traditional standardized achievement tests and cus-
tomized standards-based tests aimed at too many curricular
aims—are unable to accurately ascertain instructional quality.
And this brings us to the chapter's focus, namely, the *instructional sensitivity* of accountability tests.

WHAT IS INSTRUCTIONAL SENSITIVITY?

School leaders will find the concept of *instructional sensitivity*
useful in understanding why it is that students' scores on
some accountability tests fail to provide an accurate picture of
the effectiveness with which those students have been taught.
Here, then, is a definition of instructional sensitivity:

*A test's instructional sensitivity represents the degree to which
students' performances on that test accurately reflect the quality of instruction specifically provided to promote students'
mastery of whatever is being assessed.*

Clearly, it is more important for certain kinds of tests to be
instructionally sensitive than others. An accountability test
being used to evaluate how well a state's schools are functioning should obviously be very instructionally sensitive. In
contrast, a teacher-made test that's being used exclusively by
the teacher to assign grades to students based on a three-week
teaching unit need not be very instructionally sensitive.

Tests can range substantially in the degree to which they
are instructionally sensitive, as can be seen in Figure 5.1.
Instructional sensitivity is not an on/off variable. The degree
to which a test is instructionally sensitive is dependent on the
proportion of items on the test that are sensitive (or insensitive)
to instruction. Let's look, then, at six factors that might make
an item on an accountability test instructionally *insensitive*. If
an accountability test has few (or none) of these sorts of insensitive items, then the test is almost certain to be instructionally

sensitive. Those who develop accountability tests, therefore, should make sure their test's items do not display any of the six factors presented below.

1. Alignment Leniency

Many items on accountability tests, when judged as to their alignment with the curricular aims the items are supposed to be measuring, will be regarded as aligned with those aims (knowledge and/or skills) even if the items are only tangentially related to the curricular aim being assessed. This kind of alignment leniency can occur on two occasions. First, when an item is originally constructed, the item writer may be lax in making sure that a student's response to the item will contribute to a valid inference about the student's mastery of the specific curricular aim being measured. Second, when the quality of a set of items is being reviewed, and these days this usually occurs as part of what we describe as an "alignment study," the reviewers may be too lenient in their judgments about whether an item is suitably aligned with a curricular aim.

To illustrate, suppose there were 10 reading goals in a state's official set of content standards and that two of those goals dealt with the use of reference tools. One of those reading goals calls for students to be able to *choose* an appropriate reference tool (such as a map, a thesaurus, a bus schedule, or a

Figure 5.1 A Continuum of Instructional Sensitivity

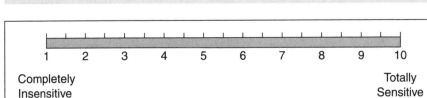

dictionary) for a given purpose. The other reading goal calls for students to be able to *use* any of the most commonly employed reference tools. There is, of course, a clear difference between selecting a suitable reference tool and employing an already-selected reference tool. Now, please consider the sample item presented in Figure 5.2. This item calls for the test-taker to use an already-presented reference tool ("the bus schedule on the adjacent page"). The item does not call for the student to choose among alternative reference tools. Accordingly, the item in Figure 5.2 should be seen as aligned with the "using" goal, but not with the "choosing" goal. Yet in many instances, the sample item would be regarded as being in alignment with *both* reading goals, that is, with the choosing goal as well as the using goal. But merely because the item in Figure 5.2 deals with a reference tool (and even if it presents an excerpt from a reference tool), this does not mean the item is aligned with both of the state's reading goals. To regard this sample item as being aligned with the choosing goal, that is, with the student's ability to select an appropriate reference tool for a specific purpose, would be a clear instance of alignment leniency.

If a teacher is attempting to promote students' mastery of a *specific* curricular aim, and the items on an accountability test fail to accurately measure students' mastery of that *specific* curricular aim, then those items will surely be unable to

Figure 5.2   A Sample Item Being Judged for Its Alignment With a Curricular Goal

Item 23

Using the bus schedule on the adjacent page, if your purpose was to determine the shortest time to reach Boston from Denver on a Monday, on which bus should you begin your journey?

  A. Bus 214

  B. Bus 197

  *C. Bus 110

  D. Bus 202

measure the success of the teacher's instructional efforts. In other words, unaligned items will most certainly turn out to be instructionally insensitive.

2. Excessive Easiness

If an item is so easy that even completely untaught students would be able to answer it correctly, then the item won't be able to distinguish between well-taught and poorly taught students. For example, consider the following item: *"How many letters are there in the word seven?"* If a student can count to five, this item poses no challenge. Clearly, because super-easy items can't distinguish between well-taught and poorly taught students, such items will be instructionally insensitive.

An Accountability Edifice Built on Pumice

Pumice is a porous form of volcanic rock. To use pumice as the foundation for a major building would be an instance of engineering idiocy. And yet, in education, we seem to have something going on that's quite analogous, and it is every bit as foolish. We have created a system of educational accountability whose conceptual cornerstone is the performance of students on annual accountability tests. If students' scores on those tests are high, it is thought educators are doing a satisfactory job. If students' score on those tests are low, it is thought educators are flopping. But, of course, a pivotal assumption in this enterprise is that the accountability tests being used are, in truth, capable of differentiating between appropriately taught and inappropriately taught students.

Educational accountability's test-based house of cards, however, should collapse in a heap if the tests being employed to evaluate educational quality are unable to do this job properly. Accordingly, wouldn't it seem sensible, given the enormous amount of money being spent on educational accountability and the enormous amount of instructional harm potentially caused by unsound decisions based on unsuitable tests, for considerable attention to have been given to the *evaluative adequacy* of the nation's educational accountability tests? But, astonishingly, such scrutiny of our accountability tests has simply not transpired. What if these cornerstone accountability tests are merely pumice pretending to be granite?

3. Excessive Difficulty

If an item is so extraordinarily difficult that even marvelously instructed students might not answer it correctly, then the item also won't distinguish between well-taught and poorly taught students. For instance, consider this italicized sample item: *"Without using your computer, what is the square root of 1,522,756?"* Because most of us have forgotten how to extract square roots of numbers from scratch—assuming we once knew how to do so—this ("no computers") sample item would be truly a difficult one for most students—and most adults. (Incidentally, the seven-digit number in the sample item is the square of 1,234.) Test items so blinking tough that even well-taught students will stumble on them also turn out to be instructionally insensitive.

4. Flawed Items

Items containing serious deficits (for example, ambiguities, garbled syntax, more than one correct answer, or no correct answer at all) will prevent well-taught students from answering the item correctly, hence making it impossible for the item to accurately distinguish between effectively and ineffectively taught students. Merely consider, for a moment, such an obviously flawed subtraction item as the following, *"When you subtract three from nine, which of the following answers do you get? (A) 7, (B) 8, (C) 5, (D) 12."* Because the correct answer (6) isn't there, can you see how such a flawed item is unable to distinguish among students according to how well they were taught? Flawed items are instructionally insensitive.

5. Socioeconomic Status (SES) Links

If an item gives a meaningful advantage to students from higher SES families, then the item will tend to measure what students bring to school rather than how well they are taught once they get there. This is a particularly insidious cause of item insensitivity. Items with SES links are often found in educational accountability tests, and such items definitely disadvantage students from lower-SES families. These items are not placed in those tests because of malevolence or elitism on the part of test developers. No, the presence of SES-linked items on important tests occurs because SES is a nicely distributed variable—a variable unlikely to change all that rapidly. Because, as you have seen, many educational achievement tests (some of which serve as accountability tests) have been constructed chiefly to provide comparative interpretations of test-takers' performances, and items linked to SES are almost certain to contribute to a test's overall score spread, SES-linked items are more common in accountability tests than might be thought.

Consider the SES-linked sample item presented in Figure 5.3, and you'll recognize how an SES-linked item can undermine the ability of an accountability test to distinguish between well-taught and poorly taught students. As you can see from the reading vocabulary item in Figure 5.3, it centers on students' understanding the meaning of the word "field." Some students, however, will come from higher-SES homes in which one or both parents are professionals, for example, attorneys, physicians, accountants, or teachers. Those parents have "a field." Lower-SES students, on the other hand, are likely to have parents who work in more menial positions. If your dad works in a car wash, and your mom cleans other people's houses, your parents have *jobs*, not *fields*. So, children from more-affluent families will, almost certainly, have heard the word "field" (as it's used in the sample item's stimulus sentence) more often than will children from less-affluent families. The SES-linked item in Figure 5.3 will give an edge to students from higher SES backgrounds. Not all high-SES kids, of course, will correctly answer the kind of item seen in Figure 5.3; nor will all low-SES children answer it incorrectly. But if we were to present this sort of item to 100 high-SES students and to 100 low-SES students, it is almost certain the more-affluent students would outperform their less-affluent classmates. SES-linked items, therefore, tend to measure the composition of a school's student body and, as a consequence, are instructionally insensitive.

Figure 5.3   An Illustrative, SES-Linked Fourth-Grade Reading
Item

> My mother's *field* is computer design.

In which of the sentences below does the word *field* mean the same
thing as in the sentence above?

   A. The pitcher knew how to *field* his position.

   B. We allowed the *field* to lie fallow.

 *C. What *field* will you enter after college?

   D. The eye specialist examined my *field* of vision.

---

6. Academic Aptitude Links

If an item gives a meaningful advantage to students who
possess greater *inherited* quantitative, verbal, or spatial aptitudes, then the item will also tend to measure what students
bring to school. As was the case with SES-linked items, in an
effort to attain the necessary score spread needed for comparative score interpretations, sometimes item writers create items
that clearly give an advantage to students who were born with
greater doses of quantitative, verbal, or spatial potentials.

These *innate* differences in human beings should not be
regarded as total limiters of what a student can accomplish in
certain fields, but it is clearly the case that a child who is born
with a big lump of quantitative aptitude will have an easier
time in math classes than will a child born with less quantitative aptitude. Let's face it: Kids are born with sometimes strik-
ingly dissimilar aptitudes. I have four children, and their
academic potentials clearly are different. My daughter is
much better verbally than are the three boys, and the boys
leave my daughter in the dust when it comes to anything
quantitative. Kids differ at birth in their academic aptitudes.

So, if you want to spread out test-takers, one good way to
do so is to include a number of *aptitude-linked* items in a test.
This is apt to provide the degree of score spread you'll need.

But the more aptitude-linked items there are on an account-ability test, the less likely it is that the test will be able to accu-rately detect instructional quality. In Figure 5.4, you will see an example of an aptitude-linked item. As you can see from this third-grade mathematics item, to answer it correctly, a student will need to employ not only quantitative abilities but also spatial and verbal abilities. To the extent that certain students will be born with higher levels of any of those acad-emic aptitudes, this item will tend to favor students who were lucky in the gene-pool lottery.

Items linked to students' inherited academic aptitudes function in much the same way that SES-linked items do, that is, students with larger dollops of inherited verbal, quantita-tive, and/or spatial smarts will tend to answer such items cor-rectly. Those students who inherited less of those academic aptitudes will tend to have more trouble with the items. When I was a beginning high school teacher, we used to call these kinds of items "IQ problems" because they presented puzzles to students, and only the smartest of our students seemed able to solve those puzzles.

Figure 5.4   A Third-Grade Aptitude-Linked Mathematics Item

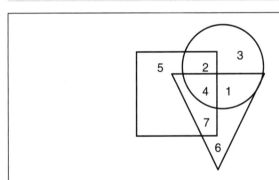

The secret number is inside the circle. It is also inside the square. It is *not* inside the triangle. Which of these is the secret number?

*a. 2   b. 3   c. 5   d. 7

All right, what can we say about the ability of accountability tests to accurately determine the instructional effectiveness of teachers? Well, the answer to this question—and to almost all questions in education—is that *it depends.* And it depends most directly on the specific accountability tests being used. I have no problem with the use of accountability tests to evaluate the quality of schooling—as long as those tests provide an *accurate* picture of how effective instruction has actually been. But when accountability tests supply misleading evidence about the quality of instruction, then a host of unsound decisions are made about how best to educate students. It is true, of course, the use of instructionally insensitive accountability tests will lead to inaccurate evaluations of educators' skills. And those inaccurate evaluations or educators are surely troubling. But what concerns me most is that the use of instructionally insensitive accountability tests *harms students.* As pointed out earlier, such tests often lead to effective instruction's being abandoned, and ineffective instruction's being retained. Instructionally insensitive accountability tests cause serious educational harm to our children.

Forty Years and Counting

The National Assessment of Educational Progress (NAEP, pronounced *nape,* as in the back of one's neck) was first administered in 1969 and has been administered periodically ever since. Because, when the topic of educational accountability arises, school leaders will sometimes be asked about this major testing program, a school leader should be at least minimally familiar with the National Assessment of Educational Progress.

The National Assessment of Educational Progress is often referred to as "The Nation's Report Card" because it is the only nationally representative, continuing evaluation of the condition of education in the United States. NAEP informs the public about what American students know and can do in various subject areas, and it compares performances of states and various student demographic groups.

(Continued)

(Continued)

NAEP is administered by the U.S. Department of Education, and is overseen by the National Assessment Governing Board (NAGB), an independent and bipartisan board made up of 26 members including governors, state legislators, local and state school officials, educators, researchers, business representatives, and members of the general public. NAGB members are appointed by the U.S. Secretary of Education.

It is often thought that there is only a single NAEP, but actually this testing program includes two fairly different operations. *Main NAEP* assessments are administered periodically using frameworks that change about every 10 years to reflect current approaches to instruction and measurement. Components of Main NAEP include *National NAEP* assessments that provide results for students in Grades 4, 8, and 12 in reading, mathematics, writing, science, U.S. history, geography, and other subjects; *State-by-State* assessments which began in 1990 and are administered to students in Grades 4 and 8 in reading, mathematics, writing, and science; and *Trial Urban District* assessments that, starting in 2002, report on the achievement of Grade 4 and 8 students in about 20 urban school districts that voluntarily participate in assessments of reading, mathematics, writing, and science. But there is, in addition to Main NAEP, *Long-Term Trend* assessments, administered since the early 1970s. Long-Term Trend assessments are given every four years to students at *ages* (not grades) 9, 13, and 17 in reading and mathematics.

Because NAEP is administered to students using a sophisticated *matrix sampling* system whereby a carefully chosen *sample* of students takes a *sample* of the test's items, it is impossible to arrive at an individual test-taker's score. Moreover, scores are not provided for schools or for school districts (other than those urban districts that have volunteered to take part in the Trial Urban District Assessments). Accordingly, in its current form, NAEP could obviously not be used to reach accountability-related evaluative judgments about individual schools or districts.

Although, when the architects of national assessment first conceptualized this assessment program back in the mid-60s, the idea that it would be used in any sort of national accountability program was roundly rejected, we currently see many educational policymakers regarding NAEP as the "gold standard" which can be employed to determine if state-specific accountability tests are suitably stringent. If, for example, a state's own accountability tests indicate that far more of the state's students are "proficient" than is indicated by NAEP, then questions arise regarding the suitability of the state's accountability tests or the state-set performance standards for "proficiency."

If for no other reason than to avoid appearing uninformed regarding the nature of this long-standing national assessment activity, school leaders could find worse ways to waste time than to consult the informative Web site available at www.nationsreportcard.gov.

DETERMINING AN ACCOUNTABILITY TEST'S INSTRUCTIONAL SENSITIVITY

Just as you saw in the previous chapter regarding the detection of assessment bias, two different strategies can be employed in ascertaining the degree to which an accountability test is instructionally sensitive, that is, a *judgmental* strategy and an *empirical* strategy. Without going into great detail about the particulars of those two approaches, here is generally how each of those strategies function.

Judgmental Appraisals

To judgmentally appraise an accountability test's instructional sensitivity, all we need to do is ask a group of seasoned educators to review a test's items, one at a time, to discern if there are any qualities in those items apt to make them instructionally insensitive. This item review might take place at the same time an accountability test's items are being reviewed on other grounds, for instance, when a test's curricular alignment or assessment bias is being judged. All that's necessary to do is orient the reviewers to the nature of instructional sensitivity, then familiarize them with factors (such as the six identified earlier in the chapter) that might cause an item to be instructionally insensitive. At this point, reviewers would be given the items to be reviewed as well as a designation (and a description) of the curricular aim dominantly being assessed by each item. Reviewers would then be asked to answer a question such as the following regarding each item being reviewed.

If a teacher has provided reasonably effective instruction related to the curricular aim measured by this item, is it likely a substantial majority of the teacher's students will respond correctly to the item?

A "No" answer from a reviewer would mean that if a student had been taught with reasonable effectiveness to master the curricular aim measured by this item, many of the teacher's students would *not* be able to respond correctly to the item. Put simply, a "Yes" answer to the review question signifies that a reviewer thinks well-taught students will tend to answer the item correctly and poorly taught students will tend to answer the item incorrectly. A compilation of how many items on an accountability test are judged by the review group to be instructionally insensitive will provide a useful estimate of the instructional sensitivity of the test.

Judgmental appraisals of an accountability test's items with respect to their instructional sensitivity are relatively inexpensive (especially if carried out in concert with other item-review activities). Such reviews can lead not only to the deletion of items regarded as instructionally insensitive but can also supply those concerned about the test's use with a carefully obtained estimate of the degree to which a test's items are likely to be sensitive to instructional quality.

Empirical Strategies

Again, patterned after the approach used in the detection of assessment bias whereby the per-item performances of different groups of students are contrasted, the same empirical strategy can be employed here, but with some significant variations. Although exploratory empirical studies of instructional sensitivity have been initiated in several parts of the United States, our knowledge of how best to carry out such studies is, at the present, meager. School leaders, however, should understand the essence of how an empirical strategy for detecting of instructionally insensitive items might work.

First off, it will be necessary to identify a group of "effectively taught" students and a group of "ineffectively taught" students. In many settings, this requirement may be difficult, if not impossible, to satisfy. However, in any setting where students' mastery of the same skills are assessed in adjacent grades—and assessed with at least a small cluster of items—it would often be possible to identify two groups of definitely different students. *Group One* would consist of students who had not mastered a particular skill in the previous school year but had mastered that same skill during the subsequent school year. *Group Two*, in contrast, would consist of students who had not mastered this particular skill in either of the two consecutive years. It seems reasonable to regard students in Group One as having been taught more effectively than students in Group Two.

If, then, we can identify teachers who are able to get the bulk of their students to be classified in Group One, we should be able to identify those items that are able and unable to detect these skill-specific improvements over a one-year span. Whether this sort of approach needs to be focused on changes in students' mastery of one curricular aim at a time, or can be used for larger collections of curricular aims, is an empirical question that must be answered.

Empirical studies of items' instructional sensitivity—even though methodologically immature at the moment, might be used in concert with judgmental studies of items' instructional sensitivity. The procedural particulars of empirical approaches to the detection of an item's instructional sensitivity must surely be refined, but early tryouts of this methodology are encouraging.

WHAT'S A SCHOOL LEADER TO DO?

As you can see, instructionally insensitive accountability tests can have a very direct impact on any school leader. So, what should a school leader do about this significant issue? Well, first and most important, you need to discover how instructionally sensitive the accountability tests are that have the most bearing on your own work. This may be tougher to do than it might seem. Few of today's educational accountability tests have been systematically analyzed to determine how many instructionally insensitive items they contain. So, what you need to find out is *whether* the accountability tests that affect your work have ever been formally scrutinized on the basis of their ability to elicit accurate evidence of instructional sensitivity. If you find that this has not been done, then you simply can't determine the degree of instructional sensitivity present in the tests about which you are concerned. Were I a school leader in such a "can't tell" setting, I'd probably conclude that the accountability tests most likely are instructionally insensitive. After all, if no formal appraisals of a test's instructional sensitivity have been carried out, this suggests that those who created the test were not particularly concerned with the idea that an accountability test needs to accurately detect the quality of instruction.

Think back, for a moment, to the nature of assessment validity as set forth in Chapter 2. If policymakers are relying on test-based inferences to evaluate school quality, isn't it imperative that we supply solid evidence that our accountability tests can effectively carry out this evaluative mission? But, astonishingly, *such validity evidence does not exist* for today's ubiquitous accountability tests.

What's most important about instructional sensitivity, as suggested early in the chapter, is that every school leader understands the nature of this issue well enough to explain it to others. At the moment, most of the nation's educational accountability tests have not been appraised according to their instructional sensitivity. This means that in most locales a school leader will be forced to work with accountability tests likely to be insensitive to instruction. Everything depends on the proportion of items on an accountability tests that are, themselves, instructionally insensitive. But without judgmental or empirical evidence dealing with this issue, a school leader simply can't tell.

So, if you are obliged to help others understand about the potential instructional sensitivity of an accountability test, then I encourage you to buttress your explanation, if possible, by showing examples of instructionally insensitive items taken from earlier forms of whatever accountability test is under scrutiny. Many states release a certain proportion of items every year or two from their accountability tests. Perhaps you can find a few examples in those items of one or more of the six factors treated earlier in the chapter. Look especially for items displaying excessively lenient alignment, SES links, and inherited academic-aptitude links. You need to help others understand just what instructional sensitivity is and, to the degree that your state's accountability tests include instructionally insensitive items, how instructional insensitivity can distort the accuracy of instructional evaluations. Few tactics are more potent when explaining to others about instructional sensitivity than presenting actual examples of items that, upon close inspection, turn out to be swimming in instructional insensitivity.

Finally, once school leaders understand the essentials of what's involved when an accountability test is instructionally insensitive, they really have a responsibility to try to get educational policymakers to establish procedures that will, insofar as possible, diminish the instructional insensitivity of the tests being used to determine instructional success (of lack of it). A proactive school leader who clearly sees that instructionally insensitive accountability tests will almost always end up harming students educationally (not to mention the reputations of school leaders themselves) should be talking to local board members, state board members, and legislators at all levels. Today's rampant use of untenable accountability tests will only cease when better, instructionally sensitive accountability tests are widely employed.

CRUCIAL UNDERSTANDINGS

It was suggested at the outset of this chapter that in today's educational accountability world, a school leader's understanding of instructional sensitivity can prove to be career saving. Instructional sensitivity is rarely considered as a topic in traditional textbooks dealing with educational measurement. Such omissions, however, do not diminish its importance for those whose activities are influenced by students' performances on educational accountability tests. Accordingly, the chapter's crucial understandings are not only imperative for a school leader to possess but also important for a school leader to share with others—many others.

CRUCIAL UNDERSTANDINGS

- A test's instructional sensitivity represents the degree to which students' performances on that test accurately reflect the quality of instruction specifically provided to promote students' mastery of whatever is being assessed.
- When educational accountability tests are instructionally insensitive, they often supply misleading evidence regarding the quality of schooling and, as a consequence, foster inappropriate instructional decisions.
- Educational accountability tests can be made more defensible by carefully attending to instructional sensitivity during the construction and review of a test's items.

RECOMMENDED READING[*]

Popham, W. J. (2009). *Unlearned lessons: Six stumbling blocks to our schools' success.* Cambridge, MA: Harvard Education Press.
Popham, W. J. (2011). *Classroom assessment: What teachers need to know* (6th ed.). Boston: Pearson.

---

[*] Complete bibliographic information and brief annotations are supplied for the following recommendations in the Reading Recommendations Roundup (pp. 181–190).

6

Test
Construction

Chapter 6 is about how to build educational tests. Interestingly, it is one of the shorter chapters in this book. Yet, because you're reading a book about educational testing, you're probably surprised by this up-front announcement that—in a book about testing—a chapter about test building is going to be tiny. There is, however, a reason for this apparent anomaly.

This book, as you surely know by now, was written for school leaders. Its goal is to help school leaders understand what they most need to know about educational assessment— that is, those understandings they'll need if they want to be genuinely effective school leaders. Well, for an educator to be a genuinely effective school leader, it is not truly *necessary* for that individual to understand how to construct test items or how to subsequently configure those items in tests. Putting it simply, I don't think school leaders truly need to know how to build educational tests. If, of course, a school leader wishes to become a skilled constructor of educational tests, such a skill is surely not a useless one to possess. But becoming proficient in test construction is, in my view, not an *essential, must-possess*

skill for all school leaders. Nonetheless, the two crucial understandings that will emerge from your reading the chapter are,
indeed, genuinely necessary for school leaders to possess.

What school leaders *must* possess is a general understanding of the overall test-construction process, namely, how items
are built, how they're improved, and how they are assembled
into actual tests. I'm distinguishing here between *test-
construction competence* and *test-construction understanding*.
Test-construction competence is definitely a helpful skill for
some school leaders to possess. Indeed, certain school leaders
will occasionally find themselves caught up in an activity that
definitely requires test-construction skill. But test-construction
skill is not truly mandatory for most school leaders' success.
Test-construction understanding, on the other hand, is
absolutely requisite for *all* of today's school leaders.

The reason school leaders only need to possess a general
understanding of how test items are constructed, improved,
and assembled is analogous to what goes on in many profes-
sions. Let's use an example drawn from the field of medicine.
Surgeons need not build their own scalpels—from scratch—
before tackling their surgical assignments. Most surgeons are
sufficiently effective when using equipment built by other
people—the people who specialize in, say, the creation of surgical scalpels. Besides, if surgeons were obliged to scurry out
to their garage workshops and grind their own scalpels, those
surgeons would have far less time to do lots of other important things, such as keeping abreast of key advances in their
fields of specialization. In precisely the same way, tests can be
effectively used by educators without those tests having been
constructed—from scratch—by the very same educators who
intend to use them. Test construction takes tons of time. And
few of today's school leaders tell me they are blessed with
bountiful amounts of spare time in their schedules. School
leaders need to generally understand what's involved in the
creation of educational tests, and school leaders ought to be
able to carry out reasonable evaluations of any tests they're
currently using or are even thinking about using. But school
leaders need not, themselves, be test-building maestros.

PURPOSE AS THE MEASUREMENT MOTIVATOR

The first, and most important insight a school leader must have about the way tests are built is that, when constructing educational tests, *everything should revolve around the purpose for which a test is to be used.* Some tests are intended to provide a general idea of how a student's knowledge and skills stack up against the knowledge and skills displayed by other students—such as the students in a national norm group. Some tests, as you saw in the last chapter, are supposed to help tell how instructionally effective different schools have been. Some tests are intended to help teachers diagnose students' weaknesses so those weaknesses can, after targeted instruction, be transformed into strengths. Whoever is building an educational test must start off the test-construction process by identifying the *explicit* nature of the inference or inferences that are going to be based on test-takers' performances.

To illustrate, when the purpose of a test is to supply teachers with diagnostic information about students' strengths and weaknesses, then the test developer must be sure to include enough items for each curricular aim being assessed so that, based on students' responses to a large enough collection of per-aim items, a sufficiently valid inference about a student's mastery of each assessed curricular aim can be made. If, however, the purpose of a test is to predict which students are likely to flop on an end-of-year accountability test, then such a predictive inference needs to be based on items that optimize this sort of prediction—irrespective of how may items per curricular aim the test actually includes.

As noted in Chapter 1, educational assessment revolves around the collection of evidence from which valid inferences can be made regarding students' covert status. Ideally, those inferences will consist of more than merely "nice to know" insights; rather, they will be genuinely *actionable* inferences. In other words, once the educator has arrived at test-based inferences about students, those inferences should lead to actions intended to benefit the students who were tested. It is for this reason that *purpose* overshadows everything else when tests are being built. It is the nature of this purpose—ideally framed in the form of the actionable inferences based on students' performances—that ought to govern all aspects of the test-development game. If school leaders can focus on the specific decisions to be influenced by test-takers' performances, then clarity regarding the assessment's real purpose usually follows.

A THREE-COMPONENT GAME PLAN

A school leader needs to see the big picture when it comes to test construction—even though the specific details of that big picture need not be mastered. Presented in Figure 6.1, therefore, is a graphic representation of the three major operations involved when an important educational test is to be built. As you can see, the *purpose* of the assessment influences all three aspects of the test-construction process. In turn, then, we see that the three major operations involved when constructing an education assessment are (1) *item development,* (2) *item improvement,* and (3) *test assembly.* Each of these steps is always required when any sort of significant educational test is created. Of course, for certain sorts of less significant teacher-made tests, some of these steps are given short shrift. I know many teachers who will whip up quizzes covering short-duration instructional sequences, yet never spend time trying to improve the quiz items or thinking carefully about how to arrange them in a test. That's understandable; when low-stakes classroom tests are being built, all three operations seen in Figure 6.1 need not be undertaken.

But, as depicted in Figure 6.1, sensible developers of any sort of *significant* educational assessment should always be influenced by the purpose for which the test is to be constructed, that is, influenced by the inferences (hopefully actionable) to be made on the basis of test-takers' performances. First, as you see, the items themselves are to be developed. The nature of these items can range from the most

Figure 6.1 The Three Purpose-Governed Operations in the Development of Important Educational Assessments

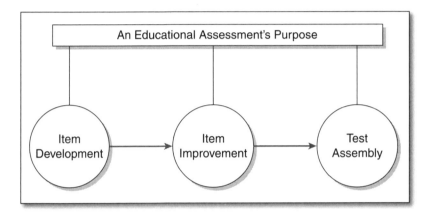

traditional sorts of paper-and-pencil items all the way to the use of computer-generated virtual worlds in which students cavort electronically while trying to solve lifelike problems. Second, once the items have been constructed, they will almost always need some sprucing up. Few item writers hit a bull's eye every time they go to the test-builder's shooting range. Fortunately, many techniques exist for improving less-than-glorious test items, and those improvement techniques come into play during the second phase of the test-construction enterprise. Finally, after the items have been devised and sufficiently polished, those items need to be assembled as an actual test. In many cases, this configuration task is quite trivial, but in some settings where high stakes are involved, this final test-assembly activity turns out to be a bit trickier.

Okay, there's the big picture. I've suggested that school leaders only need to know the general nature of what takes place in each of those three test-construction phases. The essence of each test-construction stage will be described in this chapter. Remember, this is all I think you truly need to understand. But what if *you* think otherwise? What if *you* really want to become skilled in the nuts, bolts, and fine-grained needlework of test construction? How might you do that?

Well, there are textbooks specifically written to help someone learn the tricks of the trade when building educational assessments. I've cited a few at the close of this chapter. Usually, you'll find a flock of chapters in those books dealing with such topics as the creation of selected-response items (for instance, multiple-choice or true-false items) and constructed-response items (for instance, essay or performance-test items), as well as techniques to employ when improving those items. In many textbooks dealing with educational assessment, approximately half of those books deal with the ins and outs of test construction.

Barely Trodden Assessment Arenas

For certain kinds of educational testing, we have scads of experience. When it comes to the kinds of large-scale standardized testing intended to permit comparisons among test-takers, we now have almost a full century of trying to figure out how to do this sort of assessment task properly. After all that time, happily, the educational-assessment community has learned how to do this sort of assessment job with a reasonable degree of aplomb. However, there are two assessment arenas in which our experiences are profoundly paltry. I am referring to the assessment of children with disabilities and the assessment of English language learners (ELLs).

What's important for school leaders to recognize is that, although educational-assessment personnel have been making meaningful advances in assessing students with disabilities and students' whose first language is not English, we are *really just getting under way* in understanding how best to assess these children. We'll learn more about such assessment techniques, and will be learning more as rapidly as possible, but the measurement cupboard for assessing ELLs and children with disabilities is not brimming with a host of well-studied and research-ratified procedures.

Interestingly, the most prominent push for assessment specialists to better assess these two groups of students has come directly from federal guidelines associated with federally prescribed accountability requirements. Since the enactment of the No Child Left Behind Act in 2002, for example, a figurative beehive of assessment activity has swirled abound the assessment of children with disabilities as well as ELLs.

Based on federal requirements for properly assessing these two groups, and the resultant up-tick of testing attention to those students, it is likely that as each year goes by, we will learn more about how to measure the achievement of these two groups of children.

So, school leaders need to be attentive to "breaking news" regarding how best to assess children with disabilities and ELLs. Today, we are better at this sort of assessment than we were just a few years ago. But we will know better tomorrow than we know today how to properly assess such students. Stay tuned.

Beyond reading textbooks on your own, there are also courses about educational assessment offered by most—but not all—colleges and universities. Often, these courses are especially helpful regarding the care and feeding of test items, and thus can prove beneficial to any school leader who wishes to bone up on the innards of test development. Whether by completing a formal course in educational assessment or by reading a textbook used in such courses on your own, what you'll usually be offered is a series of guidelines regarding how to create items, improve them, and toss them together. Remembering that these three operations, item building, item improving, and test assembling, are what's involved in test construction and that each of those operations must be constantly influenced by the under-development test's intended purpose, you now have the big picture of how an educational test is built. In the remainder of the chapter, I'll briefly describe the most important things that go on in each of the three test-development stages identified in Figure 6.1.

ITEM DEVELOPMENT

Just as you can't make vegetable soup without vegetables, you can't make tests without items. Typically, a test is simply a collection of items—but those ingredients may not be called "items." For example, in some language-arts tests, students are asked to display their abilities to compose original compositions by writing in response to what's called a *prompt*. But the term *prompt* is simply a synonym for *item*, and students are supposed to consider the prompt (item) and then churn out the sort of composition called for by that prompt (item).

Similarly, some teachers may rely heavily on *portfolio assessment* in which, over the course of a school term, students collect *work samples*, such as their responses to important math homework assignments or, perhaps, students' solutions to the weekly "word-problem challenges" the teacher scrawls each Monday on the chalkboard. By reviewing, over several months, how students' are progressing, teachers can often arrive at useful insights about how best to teach those students. Yet, even in portfolio assessments, there are "items." Whatever directives were employed to stimulate students' creation of the materials for those portfolios were, in fact, "items." But sometimes those items don't coincide with our traditional ideas about the way test items ought to look—the kinds of multiple-choice or essay items most of today's adults experienced while in school. But an item is whatever serves as a stimulus for a student to provide evidence that can support an inference about the student's unseen-variable status. Test items come in many costumes and, interestingly, there are specific guidelines for creating each of these item types. An educator who wishes to acquire genuine test-development expertise would need to become thoroughly conversant with all of these item-writing guidelines (also called item-writing rules or recommendations).

Shown below is an illustration of an often-advocated item-writing guideline for multiple-choice items. It is the sort of item-writing commandment frequently found in textbooks for graduate-level educational-measurement courses.

When creating answer options for multiple-choice items, never use "all of the above" alternatives, but do use "none of the above" alternatives to increase item difficulty.

As you can see, this recommendation for creating alternatives for multiple-choice items attempts to dissuade item-writers from ever employing an "all of the above" answer option, but it gives a green light to the use of a "none of the above" answer option. Typically, when an item-writing rule such as this one is provided in an educational-assessment textbook, the rule is accompanied by a rationale, an elaboration, and often examples of items that break and/or follow the rule. To illustrate, in clarifying the above item-writing rule about "of the above" answer options, it might be pointed out that as soon as the test-taker can see at least two of an item's alternatives are correct, the test-taker knows the correct answer must be "all of the above," even without having any knowledge about the correctness of the remaining alternatives. In addition, when students respond to, say, a four-option multiple-choice item and see that Choice A is correct, some of those students may immediately mark Choice A on their answer sheets without ever looking at the remaining answer options. In short, "all of the above" items can often lead to distorted pictures of what a student actually knows.

On the other hand, when a "none of the above" option is employed, this eliminates the possibility that students can choose among the presented alternatives in order to guess their way to a correct answer because it is simply the best option available. By using an elimination process, shrewd students can seem to have understood what the item is asking, but they may have really arrived at their answer through a process of weak-option estimation. To illustrate, if a four-option multiple-choice math item asks students to choose the correct answer for a double-digit multiplication problem, an astute student (but an astute student whose multiplication skills are shoddy) might choose the correct option by guesswork because, after all, one of the four answer-options *must* be correct. But by the addition (or substitution) of a "none of the above" alternative, this sort of guesswork is markedly constrained. A "none of the above" option instantly rules out the certainty that one of the item's alternatives must be the correct answer to the item's multiplication problem.

So, along with an explanation of how and why this kind of guideline should be used, readers of an assessment textbook are often told whether the guideline is based on *empirical evidence* or represents an *experiential consensus*. For some item-writing guidelines, there actually are results of empirical investigations attesting to the merits of one item-writing approach over another. For most item-writing guidelines, however, the advice embodied in a particular item-writing rule comes from the insights of seasoned item writers who, over the years, have documented what they have discovered about items that seem to work well and items that seem to stumble. In some instances, an item-writing guideline will be supported by *both* empirical evidence and the insights of past item writers. School leaders will find item-writing recommendations in all textbooks designed to support the creation defensible educational tests. Although there may be minor variations among different authors' compilations of item-writing rules, you'll encounter considerable agreement among the guidelines proffered by most authors of educational-measurement texts.

And, as noted above, examples of sample items displaying rule following and/or rule violating are often provided in those textbooks, especially for any item-writing guidelines that may be more difficult to understand. What you just encountered in the last few paragraphs about a particular item-writing guideline (the "of the above" options guideline) is what school leaders would find regarding most of the item-writing recommendations found in educational-assessment textbooks. Clearly, because there are many item-writing rules (some pertaining to each genre of item writing), and there are often subtleties associated with certain of the rules, a school leader will rarely be able to sit down with one of these textbooks, "give it a good read," and then emerge as a skilled item writer. To be a truly capable item writer, anyone—school leader or not—must put in ample reading and also plenty of practice, preferably overseen by an experienced item writer.

Are these item-writing recommendations sacrosanct? If such recommendations were followed *religiously* by item writers, would the resultant items always be marvelous? Conversely, if such recommendations were violated *irreligiously,* would the resultant items always be terrible? As you've already guessed, in item writing—as in most realms of life—such certainty is rarely encountered.

Here's the way you might think about this issue. If you had 25 tests in which the items on those tests had been developed in close accord with the item-writing rules found in just about any widely used educational-assessment textbook, and you also had 25 tests whose items had been developed without adherence to such item-writing rules, odds are that your first set of 25 "rule following" tests would be hands-down superior to the second 25 "rule flaunting" tests. In other words, the recommendation-adhering tests would be far more likely to yield evidence from which you could draw valid inferences about students. And, of course, drawing valid inferences about students is why we test those students in the first place.

So, what school leaders need to know about item writing is simply that empirical- and experience-based guidelines exist for the creation of test items, and when those rules are followed, better tests usually are created. If you want to personally become a school leader who is atypically knowledgeable regarding item-development recommendations, then you might wish to start off your quest for item-construction competence by spending time with one or more of the Recommended Reading suggestions at the chapter's close.

Two Test-Prep Guidelines

With so much attention being given to students' performances on high-stakes tests, it is not surprising that many teachers dish up some serious test preparation for their students. In some ways, this test preparation can be altogether beneficial because it can increase the validity of the inferences that educators base on students' test scores. After all, if students are required to respond to an unfamiliar type of test item, it only makes sense to help those students learn about the new kind of item and how to respond to it appropriately. The caliber of students' test performances should not be distorted by students' lack of conversance with the item types being used. So, for an upcoming test featuring any sort of *atypical* assessment procedures, a reasonable amount of test preparation usually leads to more-accurate appraisals of students' abilities and, as a consequence, yields more-valid inferences about those abilities.

(Continued)

(Continued)

But because most educators have not devoted serious thought to what kinds of test-prep practices are appropriate and what kinds are not, school leaders may find it useful to familiarize their colleagues with the following two guidelines that, if followed, will ensure that a teacher's test-prep activities are appropriate. In turn, then, here are *the professional-ethics guideline* and *the educational-defensibility guideline*. Each guideline, having been identified below, will be briefly described.

The Professional-Ethics Guideline: *No test-preparation procedure should violate the ethical principles of the education profession.*

All professional groups have identified profession-specific rules that should govern their members. In education, because a teacher is to function *in loco parentis*, that is, in place of a child's parent, it is apparent that teachers must model appropriate behaviors for their students. Thus, if a teacher were to give students more than the prescribed time to complete a standardized test, or if a teacher supplied some students—during the test—with the correct answers to tough questions, such teachers would clearly be cheating and, as such, would be engaging in conduct in violation of the ethical principles of the education profession.

The Educational-Defensibility Guideline: *No test-preparation procedure should increase students' test scores without simultaneously increasing students' mastery of the curricular aim represented by that test.*

This second guideline is often violated these days by teachers who are desperate to see their students' test scores improve. Some test-prep activities are really aimed at getting students to perform well on a particular set of items, not to master the skills and/or knowledge on which those items are based. The often-used phrase, *teaching to the test*, adds confusion, not clarity, to this issue. When *teaching to the test* means a teacher is supplying instruction aimed at getting students to master the skills and/or knowledge on which a test is based, then this sort of test-related teaching is quite appropriate. However, when teachers merely strive to get students to do well on a particular set of items, then such test prep would clearly violate the educational-defensibility guideline.

What's most important when school leaders are confronted with the test-preparation issue is that serious consideration be given to what's okay and what's not okay. The two guidelines presented above can be considered at some length by educators and then applied with considerable zeal.

ITEM IMPROVEMENT

The essence of what a school leader needs to know about the improvement of items is that two general approaches exist for doing so, a *judgmental strategy* and an *empirical strategy.* One or both of these methods may be employed to improve test items, and their use depends almost directly on the significance of the tests under development.

Judgmental item improvement occurs when already developed items are scrutinized for quality by individuals other than the original item writers. It should be noted that for many of today's high-stakes accountability tests, most items are created by freelance item writers who are paid for each acceptable item by a test-development firm that's creating the test. In all such instances, or at least all instances I've ever heard about, these freelance items are then reviewed by editors in the firm commissioning the freelancers. Most of the larger test-development companies also have staffs of their own, in-house item writers. But if the numbers of test items being developed are larger than usual, then both in-house and freelance item writers (often teachers or former teachers) are used to generate sufficient items. The more significant the tests are, the more reviewers or editors there usually are who will be called on to evaluate the under-development items.

What do these editors look for as they evaluate items? Well, not surprisingly, they typically see if the items adhere to the very same collection of item-writing guidelines to be followed when items are originally built. If early-version items violate one or more of these generally approved item-writing guidelines, the editors typically try to massage any offending items so those items are more in line with widely accepted item-writing rules.

For some especially important educational tests, such as a state's high-stakes annual accountability tests, not only will multiple editors review draft items, but committees of experienced educators will also be formally convened to systematically appraise the items. Such review committees will be asked to see if, for example, a test's potential items are suitably aligned with the curricular aims they are supposed to be assessing. Or, perhaps, a review committee of educators will be asked to see if any items are biased against particular groups of test-takers. But, either one reviewer at a time or using officially constituted item-review panels, judgmental efforts are made to identify sickly items so that, thereafter, some first-aid assistance can be given to those less-than-sparkling items. Results of all formal item-review judgments are documented and then included in any technical reports regarding a test's quality.

In addition to judgmental item-improvement strategies, a host of *empirical* item-fixing procedures exist. Many of these have come down to us from the test-improvement procedures associated with traditional comparative-interpretation tests we've used for almost an entire century. For example, one of the important indicators of an item's performance is the item's p-value. A p-value, as you saw earlier, indicates what percent of those test-takers who completed the item answered it correctly. An item's p-value of .58, for instance, would indicate that 58 percent of those students who completed the item had answered it correctly.

One of the empirically determined qualities we've historically looked at in an item is whether those test-takers who answered an item correctly also scored well on the total test. To represent this, the item indicator used is referred to as an *item-discrimination index* and, for many decades, item-discrimination indices have been one of the chief factors used in any empirical appraisal of item quality. If students' performances on an item are positively correlated with their performances on the entire set of items for the test, then this item is said to be a "positive discriminator." Test developers typically want to include positively discriminating items because those items will contribute appropriately to a student's overall test score. If the opposite is true, so that students' responses to an item are inversely related to their performances on the total test, then the item is labeled a "negative discriminator." Historically, test developers try to include no negative discriminators on their tests because items with negative discriminations tend to be measuring something other that what's measured by the bulk of a test's items.

For significant tests, it is common to have all items *field-tested* prior to their operational use so that, based on the field test, defective items can be fixed before they are used in a "this counts" administration of the test. Either a separate field test is carried out—in advance of the first operational administration of a test—with the kinds of students for whom the items are ultimately destined, or an "embedded" field test takes place whereby field-test items are inserted in an actual operational form of a test. Once sufficient items have been tried out in separate field tests and, as necessary, improved, then most field-testing is of the embedded variety. Separate field tests are more logistically difficult to carry out and, of course, are more costly.

Again, as always, the purpose of the assessment's intended use should determine what sorts of empirical analyses are used in an effort to identify flawed items. Decisions are then made to either improve or jettison any less-than-wonderful items. Moreover, the elaborateness of any empirical field testing of items will invariably be governed by the importance of the decisions that will be riding on a given test's results.

TEST ASSEMBLY

Once potential items have been evaluated (empirically, judgmentally, or by both methods), the winning items need to be put together so they constitute an actual test. For low-stakes tests, such as most teachers' classroom assessments, this is not a particularly taxing task. Occasionally, there may be reasons to place a test's items in a particular order, for example, to avoid sequences of items in which a test's early-encountered items might give test-takers unintended clues about how to answer the test's subsequent items. But, more typically, whatever kind of configuration approach makes sense to teachers will probably do the job. Indeed, even random assignment of items to a test usually works satisfactorily. However, for particularly significant tests, the assembly of items on a test is more challenging. A school leader needs to know how the most salient of these challenges are usually addressed.

Context Effects

First off, for many kinds of items, it has been empirically established that *context effects* can make a meaningful difference in how successful a test-taker is apt to be when tackling specific items. To illustrate, suppose there were eight items on a test intended to measure a student's mastery of a particular skill. It might be the case that if one of the items were encountered first, this item would, in a very real sense, "steer test-takers in the right direction" when encountering the other seven items measuring that skill. However, if this illuminating item were placed near the end of the test, and thereby had no positive steering impact on students' interactions with the other seven items, students' performance on the entire set of eight items might plummet. Similarly, the presence of a flawed item in the early part of a test, a flawed item that turns out to have no correct answer, might not only shake students' confidence but also seriously confuse students about what it is they know and don't know. School leaders need to understand that context effects exist for many tests and for many items. Do not assume that any old configuration of test items is as good as any other old configuration. It's not so.

Equating of Test Forms

Also, because of the way today's accountability tests are being employed to track students' performances over an extended period of time, it is important that each year's accountability tests present to students the same degree of challenge as had been presented in earlier years. In other words, test forms from different years need to be *equated*. To accomplish this in each year's form of an important educational test, you will usually encounter a collection of items known as "linking items," "anchor items," or "equating items." These items will have been carefully selected so their technical properties (often referred to as their *psychometric* properties) are excellent. By using these linking items, statistical adjustments can be made in students' scores so that this year's scores represent how well a student would have performed *if this year's tests had been identical in difficulty to last year's tests*. This kind of equating can be accomplished even though many of a given year's items, other than having been field-tested, have never been used before in an operational-test form. The percent of a test's items that might be required for this equating function will range, but somewhere in the neighborhood of 15 to 25 percent of a given test's items are typically devoted to this equating mission.

The larger the proportion of items that are reused, of course, the greater will be the temptation for teachers and administrators to remember what's on a test and, therefore, to try to teach students to master the items on the previous year's test form. After all, a rather large chunk of those items, because of the need for equating, are destined to reappear on an upcoming test. And, of course, assuming there's a 20 percent reuse of last year's linking items, this gives a real edge to this year's students who have become so familiar with last year's items that they can chant those items' correct answers in choral fashion. School leaders need to be on watch for these sorts of test-preparation practices. Such memorization of previous-test practices unarguably reduces the validity of any test-based inferences regarding what students actually know and can do.

As you can see, depending on the significance and composition of a test, considerable attention must be given by test developers to the way a high-stakes test is configured. School leaders should not automatically conclude that these test-assembly decisions have been made properly. When test assembly is involved, school leaders should engage in a dash of well-warranted circumspection regarding how those test-building operations were carried out.

CRUCIAL UNDERSTANDINGS

The intent of this chapter was most definitely not to transform you into a bona fide test-construction wizard. To become that sort of school leader, you will doubtlessly need to do some serious reading, take one or more professional-development courses in educational assessment, or run across a spectacularly effective workshop for test-construction wizard wannabes. In addition, plenty of practical experience is needed in order for a school leader to pick up some genuine prowess in the particulars of test construction. No, the chapter's mission was to supply you with information from which you could arrive at the following two crucial understandings.

CRUCIAL UNDERSTANDINGS

- For constructing significant educational tests, three purpose-governed operations must be carried out: item development, item improvement, and test assembly.
- All of the major procedures to be carried out as test items are born, polished, and packaged can be appreciably enhanced by relying on experience-based or empirically proven guidelines that have been assembled over the years.

RECOMMENDED READING*

Linn, R. L., Miller, D., & Gronlund, N. E. (2008). *Measurement and assessment in teaching* (10th ed.). Upper Saddle River, NJ: Prentice-Hall/Merrill.

McMillan, J. H. (2008). *Assessment essentials for standards-based education* (2nd ed.). Thousand Oaks, CA: Corwin.

Mueller, J. (2009). *Assessing critical skills.* Columbus, OH: Linworth.

---

* Complete bibliographic information and brief annotations are supplied for the following recommendations in the Reading Recommendations Roundup (pp. 181–190).

7

Rubrics

Potentially Potent Evaluative Tools

A *rubric* is little more than a scoring guide with a fancy name. Nonetheless, a properly conceived rubric can be a tremendously useful tool for educators and, especially, for school leaders. Not all rubrics, however, are created equal. Many rubrics are so poorly constructed that their contributions are minimal or even harmful. And this is why a school leader needs to know what rubrics are, how to use them, and how to tell if a given rubric is even worth using. In this chapter, you'll learn what the essential components of a rubric are and, just as importantly, you'll learn how to distinguish between rubrics that are righteous and those that are rotten.

If a rubric is merely a gussied-up scoring guide, why don't we simply call it "a scoring guide"? Indeed, where did the ritzy label *rubric* come from in the first place? School leaders are occasionally asked where this strange term came from, so be ready to respond in a way that will suitably impress the question asker. Indeed, the word *rubric* has an interesting history that, only in the last few decades, has made it a label of importance to those engaged in educational assessment. It was not always thus.

For eons and eons, certainly when I was growing up, the term *rubric* was employed to mean a label for a *category* of one sort or another. This category-label meaning of the term came to us directly from the Middle Ages, an era during which Christian monks spent many of their waking hours copying scriptural literature by hand. At the beginning of each major new section of many of these hand-copied books, large red letters were used in an effort to alert readers to the book's upcoming new section. Because the Latin modifier for red is the word *rubrica,* in time the word *rubric* became a term used to describe a category of some sort, such as a new chapter in a medieval missal or, more generally, a classification for certain kinds of entities or phenomena. Rubrics were, back in those days, labels for category-grouped things.

But when large-scale accountability testing arrived in the United States during the 1970s, those high-stakes tests often required students to display their composition skills. Many accountability exams, sometimes taking the form of "minimum-competency tests," called for students to generate an original, on-demand composition, such as a descriptive essay or a persuasive essay. It then became necessary to score these student-written compositions. The need to hand-score thousands of students' written compositions presented an imposing challenge for the nation's testing companies. Those companies had to devise accurate, yet affordable scoring systems and then use them during massive scoring operations. During those early days of scoring hoards of students' compositions, it appears the term *rubric* was co-opted to describe the kind of scoring guide needed for these unprecedentedly large appraisals of students' written compositions.

During the last several decades, however, the label *rubric* has come to describe a scoring guide that can be used to evaluate *any* kind of constructed response produced by students— not only written materials such as essays but also student's responses to short-answer items, their oral presentations, or their participation in group-based projects. In short, we now use the term *rubric* to describe scoring guides for appraising student-generated responses to almost any kind of test item other than a selected-response item.

Because well-conceived rubrics often require their users to take sufficient time to apply those rubrics carefully, we find that today's rubrics are used primarily to help determine whether a student has mastered a relatively *high-level* cognitive skill of one sort or another. There is less need to rely on rubrics when evaluating students' mastery of low-level cognitive skills or to ascertain whether a student has acquired mastery of a body of knowledge. So, as a school leader, be prepared to run into rubrics whenever really demanding cognitive skills are being instructionally promoted.

What Makes Up a Rubric?

Three elements are always found in a well-formed rubric: (1) *evaluative criteria*, (2) *quality distinctions*, and (3) *an application strategy*. Let's look, in turn, at each of these essential features of a properly conceptualized rubric.

Evaluative Criteria

A rubric's evaluative criteria are the factors intended to determine the quality of whatever responses are being evaluated. In other words, a rubric's evaluative criteria are the things we pay attention to when arriving at a judgment about the quality of a student's response. Sometimes, other labels will be employed to describe a rubric's evaluative criteria. For example, in many sections of the United States and Canada, students' written compositions are routinely evaluated by using a "six-trait" rubric. Each of those six traits is simply what's referred to in this book as an "evaluative criterion." The traits in a six-trait rubric might include the quality of a composition's *organization*, its *content* or its adherence to the *conventions of writing*. Each of these traits (evaluative criteria) is simply one factor to which scorers of students' compositions should attend when judging a composition's quality. Other synonymous labels for evaluative criteria are sometimes employed, but you will recognize them immediately as the factors by which the quality of a student's *constructed-response* performance is to be evaluated.

Incidentally, because school leaders may often find themselves dealing in public with rubrics, and the evaluative criteria found in those rubrics, you don't want to be regarded as a leader who mangles, even mildly, important technical terms. Accordingly, please recognize that the Latin-derived word *criteria* is this noun's plural form, while *criterion* is the singular form. Thus, for instance, a suave school leader might *accurately* use the following sentence in public without being regarded by colleagues or the public as a word-wimp: "*Of the rubric's four evaluative criteria, the most important criterion was clearly the initial one.*" Remember, more than one: *criteria;* only one: *criterion.* You might be thinking, not unreasonably, this "criteria versus criterion" distinction is no big deal. And you'd be correct. But school leaders, perhaps because of the power they often hold, sometimes end up being seen by colleagues as saints or sinners. And you can be certain that some of your colleagues will surely discount your abilities if you trample a verbal nicety on which they groove. Play it safe. Get the singular/plural distinction down cold between criterion/criteria. These two words will often bubble up as a school leader romps in the world of rubrics.

If a rubric's evaluative criteria are the factors to be used in judging the quality of a students' performance, then clearly some hard thinking should go into deciding what those factors ought to be. But this hard thinking will almost always be influenced by *how many* evaluative factors should be included in a properly devised rubric? Well, because the evaluative criteria in a rubric should govern not only the *scoring* of students' skill-mastery but should also influence the *instruction* being provided to promote this skill-mastery, this is another of those many instances in which less is more. Whatever evaluative criteria exist in a rubric measuring students' mastery of a challenging to-be-assessed skill will surely be attended to by teachers as they attempt to have their students master this skill. So, not only will scorers of students' responses be benefitted by a rubric using fewer rather than more evaluative criteria, but teachers and students will also benefit.

Students as Rubric Architects?

Almost every educator who spends much time fussing with rubrics believes that students should be familiarized, as early in the instructional process as feasible, with a rubric's innards. The reason we wish students to understand what's going on in a rubric is that we want students to use a rubric's evaluative criteria as those students judge the quality of their own efforts. Rubrics can function as marvelous clarifiers of what's being sought from students.

A more limited number of educators, however, want students not only to understand what's contained in an already completed rubric but also to take an active part in originally generating the rubric. Proponents of student-built rubrics believe that when students are involved in rubric building from the get-go, those students will "own" a rubric's evaluative criteria more meaningfully and, as a consequence, will be more apt to routinely rely on that well-owned rubric when it's needed in the future.

For one basic reason, I am not a dues-paying member of the student-generated rubrics crowd. My discontent with their position begins with the recognition that rubrics should be employed to evaluate students' status with respect to mastering genuinely high-level cognitive skills, not low-level ones. Building and using rubrics for measuring students' mastery of trifling skills is not a good use of the teacher's or the students' time.

When a teacher's curricular aim calls for students to master a high-level cognitive aim, it is usually true that few of the teacher's students already possess the sought-for skill. (If students already possess the skill, then why teach it?) So, most of the students who would be called on to help decide which evaluative factors should be incorporated in a rubric will actually know little about the skill being pursued. How can students who know naught about a skill create an evaluative framework for assessing students' mastery of the yet unknown skill? The answer to this key question is that those students can't!

(Continued)

(Continued)

A teacher, of course, could explain to a class of learners what an already-chosen rubric's evaluative criteria are and why they were chosen. This is fine; and it would make good instructional sense. But such an approach does not portray students as the rubric's architects.

It is also possible for a teacher to feign student involvement in the creation of a rubric, but a rubric whose evaluative criteria have already been selected by the teacher. Students are led to believe that they are actually creating a brand-new rubric from scratch, when what they are actually doing is being steered by the teacher toward the kind of rubric the teacher wanted to use in the first place. I find phony involvement of students as a rubric's "builders" to be what it is—phony.

For students to be informed about a rubric's key features, and for those students to be given a rationale supporting the use of those features, makes ample sense. Properly constructed rubrics clarify what's being sought curricularly. But calling on ill-informed students to create a way to evaluate a skill they don't yet possess is absurd.

What we usually want as educators is for well-taught students to *internalize* important evaluative factors relevant to an upcoming task calling for the use of a particular skill. We want students to be able to *evaluate their actions themselves,* that is, to be able to judge the caliber of their own efforts. It is far easier for anyone—children or adults—to internalize and employ a handful of the most important evaluative criteria (the ones set forth in a first-rate rubric) than it is to internalize and employ a dozen or more evaluative criteria of lesser import. Teachers of composition, for example, have had considerable success in recent years when using rubrics containing only a half-dozen evaluative criteria. Going much beyond six or so evaluative criteria is rarely wise. And, if possible, using less than six evaluative criteria might even be better. Remember, for each evaluative criterion you can eliminate, this will make the remaining criteria all the more important to the students being taught how to employ those criteria when evaluating their own performances.

So, when generating a rubric's evaluative criteria, the tasks of a rubric builder are to (1) think hard about what the highest-priority factors are that should be used in judging the quality of a student's effort—always trying to keep this number as small as possible; (2) describe the essence of what is involved in each evaluative criterion, so those criteria can be used in appraising students' responses; and (3) attaching a concise label to each criterion so the labels for all evaluative criteria can be more easily employed instructionally, that is, can be more effectively taught by teachers and more readily learned by students. To illustrate the sort of rubric that might be created if a rubric builder had properly carried out these three tasks, here are the rudiments of a three-criterion rubric to evaluate the quality of a student's reading comprehension:

Evaluative Criteria for Judging Students' Reading Comprehension

Accuracy: How *accurate* is a reader's grasp and uses of what's contained in a written passage?

Relevance: How *relevant* is the passage's information being used by a reader for fulfilling the reader's purpose?

Sufficiency: Does the reader use a *sufficient* amount of the passage to suitably satisfy the reader's purpose?

A rubric containing a modest, intellectually manageable number of evaluative criteria can prove enormously useful *instructionally* because teachers can more readily get their students to acquire a meaningfully deep understanding of a small number of salient evaluative criteria rather than mastering a boxcar full of lower-significance evaluative criteria. If "less is more," then it is conversely true that "more is less."

Quality Distinctions

A second necessary component of a well-conceived rubric is a spell-out, for each evaluative criterion, of how to determine just how well a student's work stacks up against that particular criterion. Quality distinctions, therefore, allow the rubric's user to differentiate qualitatively among students' work. Putting it differently, a good rubric lets scorers know—for each evaluative criterion—how to distinguish among varying quality-levels of different students' performances. If a scorer can't tell *how to apply* a rubric's evaluative criteria when judging students' work, then what good is the rubric?

Two general approaches have been successfully employed when rubric builders supply quality-distinction guidelines for applying the rubric's evaluative criteria. Those two strategies can be described as *ordinal gradation* and *two-directional definitions.* In turn, we'll look briefly at each.

First, and most commonly, some form of *ordinal gradation* is used to distinguish among students' performance with respect to each evaluative criterion. An "ordinal" system is one that expresses degree or quality in an ordered series such as "best," "next best," and "worst." In ordinal systems, the difference between the system's categories need not be equal (such as is usually assumed when we count the number of correct answers a student makes on a test—so that 20 correct is thought to be twice as good as 10 correct). Typical ordinal-gradation systems in rubrics rely on numbers of points awarded on the basis of the frequency (or gravity) of students' mistakes. Points can also be awarded based on the frequency (or grandeur) of the positive elements in a student's response. Consider, for example, the following ordinal-gradation strategy for judging a student's satisfaction of the "written mechanics" evaluative criterion in a rubric for scoring students' written compositions. As you can see, the ordinal categories in this example are linked to the number of a student's missteps:

An Illustrative Ordinal-Gradation Approach to Quality Distinction

Evaluative Criterion: *Written Mechanics:* The following points are to be awarded on the basis of the number of clear-cut errors in spelling, punctuation, and capitalization found in a student's composition:

4 Points	*Zero to two errors*
3 Points	*Three to five errors*
2 Points	*Six to eight errors*
1 Point	*Nine or ten errors*
0 Points	*More than ten errors or "off-topic," that is, not responsive to the task given*

In addition to being based on the number of points to be awarded, an ordinal-gradation scheme can also employ ordered labels such as *weak, average,* and *strong.* A commonly used ordinal-gradation approach to distinguishing among students' performance levels it to place students' responses in the following ordered categories: "below basic," "basic," "proficient," or "advanced." If an ordinal-gradation strategy using such labels as *basic* is employed (rather than numbers of errors such as in the above example for written mechanics), the rubric's builders must describe which factors will make a "basic" quality response, for example, make a student's response truly different than a "below basic" quality response. Clearly, the excellence of a rubric will hinge heavily on the clarity with which the quality distinctions for its evaluative criteria have been spelled out.

A second approach to quality distinction for a rubric's evaluative criteria takes the form of *two-directional definitions.* In this strategy, the essence of what a rubric user should regard as students' *best work* and as their *worst work* is described, but it is described without any effort to set forth any in-between ordinal categories. Often, especially for instructional purposes, it is sufficient for teachers and students to have a general idea of what sorts of responses would, based on a particular evaluative criterion, be regarded as superior or, in contrast, be seen as inferior. (Two-directional definition rubrics are particularly useful when rubrics are used "holistically," a scoring approach to be described shortly.)

Consider the following illustration of a two-directional evaluative criterion to be used in an English class, or in a speech class, when judging the quality of students' oral presentations. One of the evaluative criteria used in the rubric is focused on the gestures used by students during their oral presentations. Note that this rubric can be used to evaluate a student's actual performance as it is taking place, rather than evaluating a student's already completed responses, such as students' compositions or their written analyses of some scientific experiment.

An Illustrative Two-Directional Definition to Quality Distinction

Evaluative Criterion: *Effective Gestures:* During a student's oral presentation, this criterion is best satisfied when students *selectively* employ appropriate gestures to emphasize points of importance without those gestures' distracting from the meaning of the point being made orally. The criterion is least well satisfied if *far too many or far too few* gestures are made during a presentation or if the *distracting nature* of the gestures employed tend to detract from the speaker's message.

As you can see, these two-directional attempts to clarify the nature of an evaluative criterion are, to be sure, considerably less precise than the ordinal-gradation approach described earlier. On the other hand, in many instances it can be argued that the more-detailed ordinal-gradation approach attempts to impose precision on the imprecise. In other words, some rubrics' ordinal-gradation strategies try to install qualitative distinctions that turn out to be more carefully delineated than can be accurately applied to real-world responses by students.

Users of rubrics should select the quality-definition strategy they deem most usable for the curricular aims and the students with whom they are working. Whichever approach is employed, however, a properly constructed rubric will always try to inform rubric users regarding how best to employ the rubric's evaluative criteria.

Application Strategy

Once a rubric's evaluative criteria have been identified, and rubric users have been shown how to apply those criteria when evaluating students' performances, the final component of a rubric is a determination of the strategy by which to apply the rubric. Rubrics, you see, can be employed either *holistically* or *analytically*. This difference is important.

When a rubric is used *holistically* to evaluate students' efforts, all of the rubric's evaluative criteria are drawn on—in concert—so the rubric user can arrive at a single, overall judgment of quality. In other words, the evaluative judgment emerging from the holistic use of a rubric is akin to an amalgam-based conclusion regarding the quality of whatever is being judged.

Although it is certainly possible to weight the importance of certain evaluative criteria so that, for instance, when a rubric user comes up with an overall, holistic judgment, the initial two evaluative criteria in a five-criterion rubric count twice as much as the remaining three evaluative criteria. In most instances, no preweighting of a rubric's evaluative criteria is imposed in holistic scoring, so the rubric user is free to "mentally weight" certain evaluative criteria. In other cases, a rubric-user is specifically directed to apply all evaluative criteria *equally*. In any case, a holistic rubric leads to an overall judgment of the student's performance that, much as we saw when using a rubric's evaluative criteria, can be rendered in the form of an ordinal judgment, for instance, employing numbers or ordered labels. Thus, for example, the holistic scoring of students' written compositions might lead to overall judgments of the compositions such as 0, 1, 2, 3, or 4.

An *analytically* applied rubric calls for the rubric user to make judgments about *each* evaluative criterion and to report those judgments on a criterion-by-criterion basis. So, if a rubric consisted of four evaluative criteria, then a student's performance would be judged separately on each of those four criteria. Although, when a rubric is employed holistically, the rubric user is typically told to "keep in mind all of the evaluative criteria" when arriving as a single, comprehensive judgment, if the rubric is employed analytically, criterion-by-criterion judgments of students' performances are made, then reported to those concerned according to each criterion.

One definite virtue of an analytic approach to the scoring of students' constructed responses is that this strategy yields patently diagnostic data, that is, students can discover on which evaluative criteria they faltered and on which evaluative criteria they flew. Teachers, too, can identify the evaluative criteria they were trying to teach but, based on students' dismal performances on those criteria, appear to be in need of being taught differently when tackled in the future. The downside of an analytic application of rubrics is that such an approach takes a scorer's time and energy. Scorers can roll through many more students' responses when using a holistic approach than when using an analytic-scoring scheme. This time-saving dividend is a nontrivial advantage for the use of holistic scoring. In some instances, all responses in a set of students' papers are first scored holistically, and only then are the lowest overall responses rescored analytically. The advantage of the second scoring, of course, is that it yields diagnostic data for the students most in need of additional instruction. Based on the analytic scoring, more fine-tuned instruction can be provided by teachers to those students who most need it.

Furniture of the Mind

A good friend, Ernie Rothkopf, once told me that professionals behave "as a function of the furniture of their offices." He illustrated his point by saying that, for example, educators rely on whatever equipment has been provided to them in their offices, for example, a telephone, computer, printer, copying machine, and so on. We use those pieces of equipment because "they are there, yearning to be used."

Similarly, Ernie opined, people behave "as a function of the furniture of their minds." My friend argued that as soon as a person acquires a sensible way for viewing the world, for example, a powerful evaluative rubric for appraising one's own oral presentations, then that person will rely on this "mental furniture" to guide the organization and delivery of future oral presentations. And this is why, of course, well-formed rubrics can be so powerful in influencing students' behavior. Properly conceived evaluative rubrics can, indeed, become the analytic furniture of our minds.

Educators must be wary, however, of piling too many rubrics on their students. Astute teachers will engage in some serious rubric prioritization so that students become facile in employing those rubrics dealing with the most important cognitive skills they will need. If students are asked to master too many rubrics, they may end up mastering none. After all, if someone puts too much furniture in your office, you might never get the door open.

These three operations, then, must be carried out when creating a rubric, namely, (1) identifying the rubric's evaluative criteria, (2) determining how to use those criteria when judging students' performances, and (3) deciding whether to apply the rubric's criteria holistically or analytically. However, while educators are completing those three tasks, it is possible to go seriously haywire, that is, to create next-to-worthless rubrics. School leaders, therefore, need to identify two dysfunctional kinds of rubrics that, regrettably, are frequently found in today's schools. Let's close out the chapter by looking at three kinds of rubrics, only one of which is capable of improving the quality of schooling.

DETERMINING A RUBRIC'S QUALITY

School leaders must recognize that some pretty shabby rubrics are currently cavorting in our schools. School leaders should be able to identify two kinds of loser rubrics and one kind of winner rubric. School leaders need to understand how

to readily distinguish among these three species of rubrics—
two of which *should* be endangered.

Hypergeneral Rubrics

One kind of largely useless rubric can be aptly charac-
terized as a *hypergeneral* rubric. A hypergeneral rubric's
evaluative criteria are inexact, often vague, and simply too
general for rubric users to really apply those criteria with
any sort of judgmental rigor when scoring students' responses. Moreover, when a rubric's evaluative criteria are too
squishy, so teachers can't grasp what those criteria truly
mean, then teachers will clearly be unable to communicate
to students what the rubric's evaluative factors actually are.
Any time the creator of a rubric tries to generate evaluative
criteria that will be applicable to everything in sight, the
rubric's utility typically takes a hike.

Bob Marzano, a friend and a colleague whose work I usually applaud with enthusiasm, has unfortunately developed a
generic rubric he claims can be applied to all content areas
(Marzano, 2008, p. 10). I think, unfortunately, that in this
instance my friend erred. His rubric first sets out a score of 3.0,
indicating that, "There are no major errors or omissions regarding any of the information and/or processes (simple or complex) that were explicitly taught." Thereafter, a top score of 4.0
is given when, "In addition to Score 3.0 performance, the
student demonstrates in-depth inferences and applications that
go beyond what was taught." Lower scores on this hypergeneral rubric are earned by subtracting from the 3.0 scores. For
instance, a score of 2.0 is assigned when "There are no major
errors or omissions regarding the simpler details and processes,
but there are major errors or omissions regarding the more
complex ideas and processes." A complete nine-level rubric
emerges from this analysis (Marzano, 2008, pp. 10–14). But
when one considers this scoring guide carefully, the rubric is
really of little help to those who need to score students' work or
who need to teach students how to evaluate their own performances. Hypergeneral rubrics, because they must be devised in

a manner that will allow them to work in a wide variety of settings, attempt to become one-size-fits-all scoring guides wherein acceptable performances are deemed to be largely error free, better performances hinge on often undefined student insights, and worse performances embody additional errors. Most hypergeneral rubrics remind us of the traditional, typically ill-defined grading scales that teachers sometimes employ to dish out grades to their students. Hypergeneral rubrics, though well intentioned, are fundamentally feckless.

Task-Specific Rubrics

A second sort of useless rubric is seen when a rubric's focus is on evaluating a student's response to the particular assessment task the student has been given. In many types of educational assessments, a student is asked to respond to a specific task, for example, to write a narrative essay about a real-world series of events in which the student took part—such as a field trip to City Hall to watch an open hearing about renaming a city street after a famous minority person, in this illustrative instance, Cesar Chavez. What the teacher wants students to be able to do is to become skilled in their ability to supply story-like compositions recounting the chief events of such occurrences. That's the skill involved—the students' being able to write crackerjack narrative compositions.

But what if the rubric that's to be used by a teacher is organized not around the narrative-writing *skill* but, rather, about the test-taker's skill displayed *in this specific instance*? Let's say, for example, the rubric includes an evaluative criterion in which a student's essay is required to incorporate several specific facts about Cesar Chavez' accomplishments as a labor leader—facts that were presented during the open hearing at City Hall. A task-specific rubric, of course, makes it relatively easy to score students' responses to the particular task involved. However, and it is a big *however*, such rubrics offer scant insight regarding how well a student has mastered the *skill* that is supposedly being employed by the student to address this assessment task. The kinds of highly particularized evaluative criteria that can help determine if a student has done well on a particular task will, sadly but truly, often have no relevance whatsoever to how well a student can accomplish *other tasks* for which the promoted skill would be required.

When we use rubrics to evaluate a test-taker's mastery of a cognitive *skill*, we typically use a particular assessment *task* to determine how well a student appears to have mastered the skill. But what we should be making an inference about is students' *skill mastery*, not their *task mastery*. And this is why, from a student's perspective, a set of task-dependent insights are of little value. Let's face it: The students may never in their lives drop in on another City Hall open hearing about renaming a street after Cesar Chavez. Task-specific rubrics composed of task-particularized evaluative criteria are of little value in promoting students' achievement of genuinely generalizable cognitive skills. And those generalizable cognitive skills are what educators should be promoting in their students.

Skill-Focused Rubrics

A rubric that can be of assistance when evaluating students' skills and, therefore, when teaching students to master such skills, is known as a *skill-focused* rubric. A skill-focused rubric's evaluative criteria set forth the important factors that can be used to evaluate students' skill mastery when responding to *any* task requiring the application of the skill being assessed. So, for instance, if students' narrative essay-writing skill is to be evaluated by asking a student to recount what went on in a City Hall open hearing, instead of an evaluative criterion dealing with particular facts regarding Cesar Chavez, an evaluative criterion in a skill-focused rubric might deal with "whether the temporal sequence described in the student's essay accurately reflects the actual temporal sequence of the events being recounted." In a skill-focused rubric about narrative essay writing, all of the evaluative criteria in the rubric will be applicable to a student's response to *any* task calling for the student to compose a narrative essay.

What a teacher wants students to acquire when mastering a cognitive skill is an understanding of how the skill works and an ability to discern *for themselves* whether they are satisfactorily employing the skill that's being taught. A skill-focused rubric provides for students an *internalizable* evaluative template by which they can determine how successfully they are being when using the skill involved.

Although we tend to regard rubrics chiefly as ways of better assessing students, school leaders should realize that rubrics can also play a potent role in the *instruction* of students. If, early on, teachers supply students with well-crafted rubrics—presented in student-friendly language—along with examples of student work representing different levels of quality, this clarification of expectations can have a huge payoff in improved learning.

To wrap up these three types of rubrics, then, we see that two of them, namely, hypergeneral and task-specific rubrics, are of little value to educators. In marked contrast, a skill-focused rubric is of considerable evaluative and instructional worth to educators. What school leaders must recognize, therefore, is that all the positive praise received by rubrics during recent years (praise that, in the main, is definitely deserved) does not necessary mean that a particular rubric is suitable for sainthood. Some rubrics are good; some rubrics aren't.

Crucial Understandings

School leaders need to recognize that whenever educators ask students to generate their own responses to assessment tasks (and those tasks can include any sort of constructed-response test items), it is necessary to score students' responses. Because constructed-response items can be effectively employed in measuring the degree to which students have mastered signif-icant cognitive skills, rubrics will typically be employed to determine how effectively students have mastered a given skill. Thus, it becomes apparent that all school leaders need to possess reasonable conversance with what rubrics are, how they can be used, and how to evaluate the quality of a given rubric. The following two crucial understandings, then, are the ones to be taken away from this chapter.

CRUCIAL UNDERSTANDINGS

- The three essential components of a rubric, that is, a scoring guide, are (1) the evaluative criteria by which a student's performance is judged, (2) guidance regarding how those criteria are to be used to determine the quality of a student's performance, and (3) an application strategy calling for the use of holistic scoring, analytic scoring, or a combination of both.
- Although a skill-focused rubric can be of enormous use to educators, hypergeneral or task-specific rubrics are of limited utility.

RECOMMENDED READING[*]

Glickman-Bond, J., & Rose, K. (2006). *Creating and using rubrics in today's classrooms: A practical guide.* Norwood, MA: Christopher-Gordon.

Popham, W. J. (2006). *Mastering assessment: A self-service system for educators.* New York: Routledge.

---

* Complete bibliographic information and brief annotations are supplied for the following recommendations in the Reading Recommendations Roundup (pp. 181–190).

8

Formative Assessment

Underused Magic Bullet

S chool leaders need to know what *formative assessment* is—and what it isn't. School leaders also need to know that formative assessment can dramatically improve the caliber of kid learning. Finally, school leaders need to know how to get more teachers to use formative assessment—and then make sure those teachers do.

Before dipping into formative assessment per se, however, I want you to engage in a brief, two-part thought experiment. *Please!* For Part I, please imagine that members of the pharmaceutical industry have discovered a low-cost, research-proven vaccine to protect young children from a life-threatening disease. Imagine further that, despite the vaccine's demonstrated ability to shield children from this deadly disease, few physicians ever urge parents to have their children vaccinated. As a consequence, thousands of young children die needlessly. How do you think the parents of those children would view the conduct of the offending physicians? How would *you* regard the conduct of those physicians?

Okay, now to Part II of the thought experiment. Suppose that in education we have discovered a low-cost, research-proven instructional process to help children learn better—lots better. Nonetheless, educators rarely use the process, advocate its use, or even inform parents of its existence. Because the new instructional process never becomes widely employed in our schools, thousands of children end up being less well educated than they should be. How do you think the parents of these inadequately taught children would view the conduct of the offending educators? How would *you* regard the actions of those educators?

Well, although the above description of flawed conduct by physicians was only make-believe, the description regarding educators' failure to employ a research-proven instructional process to help students learn better is appallingly accurate. That instructional process, a process known as *formative assessment,* is the focus of this chapter.

WHAT IS FORMATIVE ASSESSMENT?

Let's get under way with a definition of what the chapter is about.

Formative assessment is a planned process in which assessment-elicited evidence of students' status is used by teachers to adjust their ongoing instructional procedures or by students to adjust their current learning tactics.

This definition is consonant with the research evidence that supports the use of formative assessment. Conceptualizations of "formative assessment" that fail to flow from confirmatory empirical research are conceptualizations to be viewed with suspicion by sensible school leaders.

The above definition contains several significant elements, so let's look at each of them. First off, as you can see in the first few words, formative assessment is a *process.* Moreover, that process is *planned,* and it definitely doesn't spring into life serendipitously. Formative assessment, most definitely, *is not a test*. Tests are *used* during the formative-assessment process to provide evidence; but formative assessment is a planned process, not a particular kind of test. Very importantly, the formative-assessment process employs test-elicited evidence so teachers can, if they need to do so, *make adjustments* in how they are trying to teach their students. That same test-elicited evidence can also be used so students can, if they need to do so, *make adjustments* in how they are trying to learn something.

This view of formative assessment as a planned process in which assessment evidence is employed to improve teaching and learning is the only conception of formative assessment currently corroborated by research evidence. School leaders should beware of other incarnations of what some people are calling "formative assessment," but incarnations accompanied by no empirical evidence showing that, when they're used, kids learn better.

To illustrate, during the last few years, many testing companies have been hawking so-called *interim tests*, that is, standardized tests administered schoolwide or districtwide every two or three months. Many of these interim tests are being touted as implementations "of formative assessment." Indeed, enormous numbers of these interim tests, all decked out in phony formative-assessment costumes, have been sold throughout the nation. In fairness, it is certainly possible that some of these interim tests may, in fact, help teachers do a better instructional job and, therefore, benefit children. At this writing, however, there is *no evidence* to convincingly support instructional payoffs from the use of the interim tests—interim tests that many educators have been mistakenly told are formative assessments. Indeed, based on the research evidence we now have at our disposal, and relying on a definition of formative assessment akin to the one presented at the outset of the chapter, it is a flat-out mistake to even use the phrase, *formative assessments*. Assessments are not formative. Rather, the *results* of an assessment are central to the formative-assessment *process*. But a test itself is not formative.

In truth, because teachers have recently been pounded—almost relentlessly—with an "improve scores" measurement mallet, many teachers have understandably come to resent anything even *remotely* associated with testing. In retrospect, it was probably unwise to use the label "formative *assessment*" as a way of describing this powerful *instructional* process. It would most likely have been better to refer to the formative-assessment process simply as an *evidence-informed* approach to instructional decision making—an approach in which the appropriateness of a teacher's instructional decisions hinges on how well students have learned what they're supposed to have learned. To determine how well students have learned what they are supposed to have learned, we simply collect evidence by using assessment techniques of one sort or another. Formative assessment, then, should really be thought of as a defensible approach to *instruction* that, based on the assessment-garnered *results* of the instructional activities being used, might incline teachers or students to adjust what they are currently doing.

WHAT EVIDENCE SUPPORTS FORMATIVE ASSESSMENT?

In an important 1998 research review, two British researchers, Paul Black and Dylan Wiliam, identified almost 700 published studies dealing with classroom assessment. They then painstakingly analyzed about 250 of the most carefully conducted of these investigations. The 250 studies under analysis covered about a 10-year period. Results of their thoroughgoing, transparently explicated review indicated that

> The consistent feature across the variety of these examples is that they all show that attention to formative assessment can lead to significant learning gains. Although there is no guarantee that it will do so irrespective of the context and the particular approach adopted, *we have not*

come across any report of negative effects following on an enhancement of formative practice. (Black & Wiliam, 1998a, pp. 11–12, emphasis added)

This strong support of formative assessment—that is, the formative-assessment process as defined earlier in the chapter—is consistent with the chief conclusions of two earlier reviews of research dealing with classroom assessment (Crooks, 1988; Natriello, 1987). Nor were the learning gains for formative assessment reported in the Black and Wiliam review merely trifling ones. As these two researchers pointed out, the student gains in learning triggered by formative assessment were among the largest ever reported for instructional innovations. Indeed, the gains "are larger than most of those found for educational interventions" (Black & Wiliam, 1998b, p. 141). A particularly impressive conclusion of the Black and Wiliam review is that the formative-assessment process is sufficiently robust so that it can be carried out by teachers in a variety of ways yet still lead to substantially improved learning for students. As these two British scholars observed, "Significant gains can be achieved by many different routes, and initiatives here are not likely to fail through neglect of delicate and subtle features" (1998a, p. 61).

So, a quick look at the Black of Wiliam review, as well as the conclusions of earlier reviews, reveals that the formative-assessment process works, it works big time, and it can be used in a variety of ways to improve students' learning. Black and Wiliam caution us, however, that formative assessment cannot merely be a peripheral sort of add-on to "instruction as usual." As they point out, "the changes in classroom practice are central rather than marginal, and have to be incorporated by each teacher into his or her practice in his or her own way" (1998a, p. 62). Putting it differently, after carefully reading the seminal 1998 research review by Black and Wiliam, most people come away with the clear impression that, when properly implemented, the formative-assessment process can become, for many teachers, a substantially new way of thinking about instruction. And it is for this reason that today's school leaders need to be really conversant with the innards of formative assessment—it is a new way of thinking about instruction, and it most definitely works!

Who Needs Evidence Anyway?

Those who advocate the use of formative assessment are in the wonderful position of pushing for adoption of a process that's been well supported empirically. We can now find, after all, a boatload of well-designed studies showing that formative assessment will benefit students. But *even if there were not a solitary scrap of evidence to support formative assessment*, teachers should still use this process, and use it with confidence.

Let's face it: The formative-assessment process sits on a sack full of good sense. Teachers exist in order to promote changes in their students, that is, to get their students to acquire important skills, knowledge, and affective dispositions (as you'll see in Chapter 9). But it typically takes time for students to achieve the curricular aims a teacher has set out for those students, and in most instances there is some serious en route learning that must be mastered by students.

Well, to find out if students have or haven't mastered the en route things they need to master, the formative-assessment process simply directs teachers to collect *evidence* regarding students' current achievement status. Such evidence is obtained via some sort of assessment—often formal, but sometimes informal. If this assessment-elicited evidence indicates that the instruction is going well, the teacher keeps doing what's been working. If the assessment-elicited evidence indicates students are not learning as well as had been hoped, then the teacher either makes adjustments in immediately upcoming instructional activities and/or urges students to adjust their own leaning tactics.

Put simply, formative assessment directs teachers to judge the quality of their instruction by collecting evidence about its effects on students. The teacher who is formatively oriented, therefore, constantly judges the effectiveness of instruction by attending to its consequences and makes any necessary adjustments based on assessment-collected evidence. Is it *really* necessary to bolster such a common-sense stance with a bevy of empirical investigations? Formative assessment makes so much intuitive sense that it really needs no research sanctification.

How Does Formative Assessment Function?

If you revisit the definition of formative assessment on page 138, you'll see that this process takes place when test-elicited evidence of students' status is used *either* by teachers to adjust their ongoing instructional activities *or* by students to adjust their current learning tactics (that is, the ways those students are trying to learn something). Thus, formative assessment takes place when *teachers* use assessment results to shape up their own teaching, but it also takes place when *students* use assessment results to shape up their own learning procedures. Formative assessment, to be sure, is also present when *both* of these activities are going on simultaneously. The Black and Wiliam research synthesis supports these three applications of formative assessment.

Four Levels of Formative Assessment

Because there are two potential sets of players (teachers adjusting instruction and students adjusting learning tactics), it is often confusing to squish those two players' actions together. Moreover, because there are substantially different ways in which formative assessment can be implemented, it can quickly become confusing if we regard one variant of formative assessment as identical to another variant. Accordingly, it may be useful for school leaders to consider the four *levels* of formative assessment seen in Figure 8.1. As you can see in the figure, Level 1 represents *teachers' instructional adjustments;* Level 2 represents *students' learning-tactic adjustments;* Level 3 indicates that, assuming both Level 1 and Level 2 formative assessment are in place, there is a *classroom-climate shift;* and Level 4 describes *schoolwide implementation* (that is, schoolwide or districtwide expansion in the use of formative assessment). You will note also in the figure that the four levels of formative assessment rest on the use of *learning progressions*. The four-level, one-basis view of formative assessment in Figure 8.1 can serve as a handy way for school leaders to conceptualize what can go

Figure 8.1   Four Levels of Formative Assessment Based on a Learning Progression

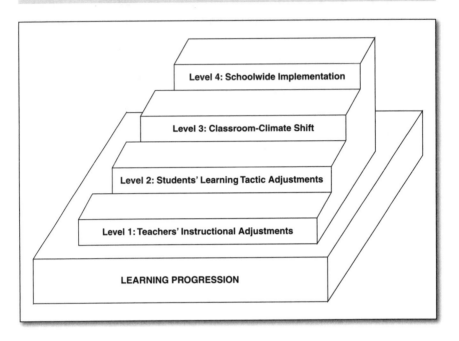

on when educators try to tangle with formative assessment. Let's briefly, then, consider each of the components in the Figure 8.1 representation of formative assessment.

Learning Progressions

Because learning progressions, as seen in the Figure 8.1 graphic, function as the foundation of formative assessment, we should probably deal with them first. A *learning progression* is a sequenced set of subskills and/or bodies of enabling knowledge it is believed students must master en route to mastering a more-remote curricular aim. We can refer to this more-remote goal students should achieve as a *target curricular aim*. The en route *subskills* or *bodies of enabling knowledge* making up the learning progression can be described as the learning progression's *building blocks*. Because, as you will soon see, these building blocks become key occasions for the collection of formative-assessment evidence, building blocks clearly play an important role in the process.

The building blocks in a learning progression represent the truly required, along-the-way learning that students *must master* in order to successfully accomplish what's set forth in the target curricular aim. Because most learning progressions are organized to help teachers and students pursue students' mastery of a cognitive skill (and it's usually a high-level cognitive skill), the building blocks in many learning progressions include *cognitive subskills*, that is, lesser cognitive skills which must first be mastered if the target curricular aim is going to be mastered by a student. But, in addition to cognitive subskills, other building blocks can consist of bodies of *enabling knowledge* that must be known by students if they are going to accomplish the target curricular aim. Each of the building blocks in a properly devised learning progression *must* be mastered by a student, or the student's likelihood of mastering the learning progression's target curricular aim will be reduced. A graphic example of a learning progression is presented in Figure 8.2, where you will see there are four building blocks, two subskills, and two bodies of enabling knowledge, all of which are regarded by those who created the learning progression as being requisite for a student's achievement of the target curricular aim. The sequence of a learning progression's building blocks represents the order in which the building blocks seem most likely to be effectively and efficiently learned by students.

As a practical matter, in a well-formed learning progression the number of building blocks should be kept as small as possible—embodying only the absolutely *required* subskills and knowledge a student needs. Because each of the building blocks in a learning progression represents something a student *must learn* in order to successfully master the target curricular aim, students' accomplishment of each building block must be verified via some form of assessment.

Figure 8.2   An Illustrative Learning Progression

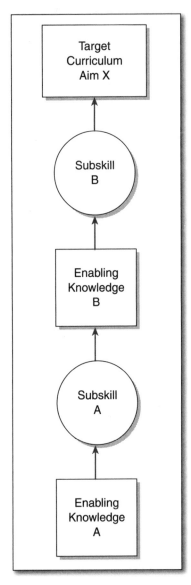

Accordingly, as the instruction aimed at each building block is about to wind down, assessment evidence is collected regarding students' building-block mastery. If too few students have satisfactorily mastered a given building block, then this warrants an adjustment in the teacher's instruction (perhaps some reteaching, but reteaching only after the teacher, hopefully, makes some instructional improvements), changes in students' learning tactics (such as employing decisively different study procedures), or alterations in *both* the teacher's instruction and the students' learning tactics. The fewer the building blocks, the less frequently will be the need for assessments and potential adjustments. It is imperative *not* to make the formative-assessment process so complicated and time consuming that teachers will be reluctant to try it out or, once having tried it, won't continue to use it. Lean learning progressions are more manageable than are lengthy learning progressions. Lean learning progressions are likely to make formative assessment flourish.

Level 1 formative assessment: teachers' instructional adjustments

Let's briefly consider each of the four levels of formative assessment by supplying you with a general notion of what's involved in each of those levels. Incidentally, if you prefer to think of the four "levels" merely as "types" of formative assessment, that's fine. Even though I have used the notion of "levels" elsewhere in a book focused exclusively on formative assessment (Popham, 2008), there is no necessary hierarchy involved in the four levels. A teacher, for instance, could attempt to install Level 2 formative assessment (students' learning-tactic adjustments) without ever having installed Level 1 formative assessment (teachers' instructional adjustments). Or, as another illustration, a school leader might employ Level 4 formative assessment (schoolwide implementation) to promote use only of Level 1 formative assessment (teachers' instructional adjustments) without ever dealing with Level 2 formative assessment (students' learning-tactic adjustments) or Level 3 formative assessment (classroom-climate shift).

When teachers carry out Level 1 formative assessment, they typically do four things, so let's lay them out as four separate steps. As a first step, teachers identify the potential occasions when they might need to adjust their instructional activities—and those occasions are linked to *each* of the building blocks in the learning progression. (Remember, for students to attain a target curricular aim, they must master all of those building blocks.) Step 2 requires the teacher to select the assessment procedures to be used in measuring students' building-block status. The assessments might be formal tests (such as actual paper-and-pencil exams) or informal-assessment procedures (such as asking students to signal their answers to a teacher's orally presented true-false questions by using a thumbs-up or thumbs-down response technique). The selected assessments are always administered *while there is still instructional time available* so that, if additional or altered instruction is warranted, there is still time to supply it. Level 1 formative assessment's Step 3 involves the teacher's deciding on "adjustment triggers," that is, choosing a prespecified quality of students' assessment performances that will dictate the need for an instructional adjustment (for instance, deciding that reteaching will be required if at least 90 percent of students did not score at least 90 percent correct on a building-block quiz). In Step 4, finally, if the assessment-elicited evidence dictates the need for an instructional adjustment, the teacher makes such an adjustment. When the performances of students on a building-block assessment are acceptable, of course, then no instructional adjustment needs to be made.

Level 2 formative assessment: students' learning-tactic adjustments

When this second level of formative assessment takes place, four steps (akin to those seen in Level 1 formative assessment) are involved, but in this case the teacher's *students are deciding* whether to adjust how they are currently tackling their learning tasks. A learning tactic is simply the way a student is attempting to learn whatever the student is supposed to be learning. Thus, Level 2 formative assessment sets out to make students become monitors of their own learning, and decision makers about whether to alter how they are currently attempting to learn something.

In Step 1 of this variant of formative assessment, students consider the most likely occasions when they might wish to adjust their learning tactics. And, because assessment evidence will ordinarily be collected by a teacher in connection with each of the learning progression's building blocks, these potential adjustment occasions typically occur when students can conveniently review the appropriateness of their current learning tactics. Step 2 calls for students to recognize that, near the conclusion of the teacher's instruction related to each building block, assessments will be administered to them—and they will be informed about the results of those assessments. In Step 3, students consider the quality of the performances they need to display if they are to stick with their current learning tactics or if they are to alter those tactics. In Step 4, students decide whether to adjust their learning tactics associated with any of the building blocks leading to mastery of a target curricular aim.

Those learning-tactic adjustments might be quite trivial, for instance, increasing the amount of at-home study time by 30 minutes a night, or quite meaningful, for instance, setting up a peer-study group that meets before school each morning to jointly review the assigned homework's major concepts. Although the four steps in Level 2 formative assessment clearly parallel the four steps in Level 1 formative assessment, the decisive difference in Level 2 is that *the student is the decision maker,* not the teacher. Accordingly, if Level 2 formative assessment is in operation in a given teacher's classroom, and some of the teacher's students use the formative-assessment process fully, while other students do not use it at all, that's the way this "student-in-charge" cookie crumbles.

Formative Assessment's Focus: It Depends

Formative assessment describes the evidence-based adjustments teachers make in their instructional procedure or the evidence-based adjustments students make in their learning tactics. So it is possible, in a given classroom, to find both teacher-focused and student-focused formative assessment going on simultaneously.

During the last several years, I have had several opportunities to work with European colleagues who, when asked to provide their take on formative assessment, almost always reply that they're mostly interested in *students'* adjustments in the ways they are trying to learn things. In other words, the European educators with whom I've discussed this issue seem to focus on getting students to become skillful monitors of their own learning progress. In the United States, however, my conversations with firing-line educators usually indicates that the way they conceive of formative assessment is chiefly as a vehicle to help *teachers* make adjustments in their ongoing instruction.

In the United States, therefore, it seems the focus of formative assessment is often on its uses in helping teachers do a better job of teaching. In Europe, however, the focus of formative assessment seems to be on helping students do a better job of learning.

Happily, this is not a zero-sum game. If formative assessment emphasizes students' using assessment evidence to adjust their learning tactics, and it works, then *students benefit.* Similarly, if formative assessment emphasizes teachers' using assessment evidence to adjust their instruction, and it works, then *students also benefit.* Either way, students win!

Level 3 formative assessment: classroom climate shift

Level 3 formative assessment calls for a striking alteration in the way most classrooms operate. What the teacher seeks when trying to install Level 3 formative assessment is a series

of fundamental changes in the atmosphere of a classroom—
changes focused on three important dimensions. First, with
respect to *learning expectations,* an attempt is made to shift *from a
belief* (by both students *and* the teacher) that substantial learning
occurs only for motivated students who possess adequate academic aptitude *to a belief* that substantial learning will take place
for all students, irrespective of their academic aptitude. The second key climate shift focuses on *responsibility for learning.* There's
an attempt made in Level 3 formative assessment to move *from
a belief* (by both students *and* the teacher) that the teacher, as the
chief instructional mover, is responsible for students' learning *to
a belief* that students must assume meaningful responsibility for
their own learning and for the learning of their classmates. A
final dimension of Level 3's classroom-climate shift deals with
the *role of classroom assessment.* In a traditional classroom, assessment is seen as a set of formal tests to be used in comparing
students and assigning grades. Well, in Level 3 formative assessment there is a shift *from a belief* (by both students *and* the
teacher) that time-honored conception of classroom assessment
to a belief that formal and informal assessments generate data to
be used chiefly for informing potential adjustments in a
teacher's instruction or in students' learning tactics.

If all three of these key shifts in classroom beliefs were to take
place, it is apparent that the result would be a whopper change
in the way traditional classrooms operate. Incidentally, in order
for Level 3's classroom-climate shift to take place, it seems almost
certain that Level 1 and Level 2 formative assessment would
already need to be up and running in a given classroom.

Level 4 formative assessment: schoolwide implementation

The final level of formative assessment deals with how best
to get formative assessment used in more classrooms. Two
general strategies have been employed to do so, one of which
seems more promising than the other. First off, there are *traditional professional-development* approaches in which multiday
workshops of presenters-plus-materials are used with educators. Such professional development is often carried out in

the hope that the words uttered orally or on paper will spur teachers to try out some variation of formative assessment. A second approach to Level 4 formative assessment calls for the use of *school learning communities,* that is, extended-duration meetings of groups of teachers and/or administrators who read about, discuss, try out, and evaluate various aspects of formative assessment.

To date, the experience of most proponents of formative assessment suggests strongly that, by far, the better of these two approaches involves the use of extended-duration school learning communities. Such groups, perhaps consisting of a dozen or so individuals, meet every few weeks to deal with a different topic related to formative assessment. During meetings of about 90 minutes—often focused on written materials (related to formative assessment) that have been read in advance by members of the learning community—a productive sharing of perceptions usually transpires regarding how best to implement formative assessment. As members of the group become more conversant with the chief elements and subtle nuances of formative assessment, some group members can actually try out certain formative-assessment techniques in their own classes, observe the effects of those techniques, then describe them to other group members during a subsequent meeting of the learning community. These sorts of real-world tryouts of formative-assessment procedures, followed by evaluative analyses by a school learning community, are often particularly illuminating for the group's members. Clearly, what's being sought in a well-conducted school learning community is greater understanding on every member's part regarding how best to employ formative assessment so this process optimally benefits students.

Once Over, Very Lightly

Formative assessment is an enormously powerful classroom process that improves students' learning. This chapter, as you recognize, provided only a very quick dip into the process.

All school leaders need to comprehend the handful of crucial understandings emerging from the chapter. But *some* school leaders need to learn more about formative assessment, *much more* than what's set forth here. This is because the formative-assessment process is so effective, that is, it's so blinking beneficial for students, some of us need to promote its widespread use with genuine fervor.

Fortunately, as every year goes by, we find more and more materials becoming available regarding formative assessment. Recently, I wrote a book dealing with formative assessment (Popham, 2008), and it definitely discusses formative assessment more extensively than what's in this chapter. But other excellent written and video resources dealing with formative assessment are being released almost monthly. At least some school leaders need to become really familiar with formative assessment's innards so that they can play a leadership role in getting this *instructional* process more widely employed. After all, isn't playing a leadership role what school leaders are supposed to do?

Crucial Understandings

As is true in the other chapters of this book, it is often challenging to isolate the most important understandings associated with whatever topic has been treated in the chapter. Nonetheless, the following two crucial understandings seem to capture the insights that today's school leaders must internalize regarding formative assessment.

Crucial Understandings

- The formative-assessment process revolves around the collection of assessment-elicited evidence regarding students' learning, such evidence then being used by teachers to make adjustments in their ongoing instruction or by students to adjust their current learning tactics.

> • Although compelling evidence shows that formative assessment will decisively improve students' learning, educators must be wary of commercially promoted programs that, though claiming to be "research-proven formative assessment," are actually imposters.

RECOMMENDED READING[*]

Black, P., & Wiliam, D. (1998a). Assessment and classroom learning. *Assessment in Education: Principles, Policy and Practice, 5*(1), 7–73.

Black, P., & Wiliam, D. (1998b). Inside the black box: Raising standards through classroom assessment. *Phi Delta Kappan, 80*(2), 139–148.

Crooks, T. (1988). The impact of classroom evaluation practices on students. *Review of Educational Research, 58*(4), 438–481.

Heritage, M. (2010). *Formative assessment: A process for improving learning.* Thousand Oaks, CA: Corwin.

McMillan, J. H. (Ed.). (2007). *Formative classroom assessment: Theory into practice.* New York: Teachers College Press.

Natriello, G. (1987). The impact of evaluation processes on students. *Educational Psychologist, 22*(2) 155–175.

Popham, W. J. (2008). *Transformative Assessment.* Alexandria, VA: Association for Supervision and Curriculum Development.

---

[*] Complete bibliographic information and brief annotations are supplied for the following recommendations in the Reading Recommendations Roundup (pp. 181–190).

9

Assessing Students' Affect

If students arrive in a school's kindergarten totally unable to read and several years later have not only learned to read rapidly but can read with genuine comprehension, then the school's teachers should surely be applauded for their instructional success. But this success is definitely in the *cognitive* arena. What if those same students, the children who became such good readers, simply *hate to read?* In other words, what if those students' attitudes toward reading are altogether negative? The kids can read, but they don't want to do so. Whatever the school's teachers did to promote their students' cognitive mastery of reading has apparently soured those same students on the very thing they are good at. Do the school's teachers still warrant our unbridled applause? Perhaps a bit of bridling is in order.

This chapter is focused on the measurement of students' *affect*, that is, students' *attitudes, interests,* and *values*. We'll be looking at why educators should measure students' affect, a general strategy for assessing students' affect, and then how to actually construct the kinds of measuring instruments that can be employed to collect evidence regarding students' affect.

WHY MESS AROUND WITH AFFECT?

But why, you might ask, should educators even care about students' affect? After all, aren't today's expectations of educators wrapped more tightly around cognition than affect? Aren't today's teachers supposed to focus on only one thing, namely, boosting students' performances on cognitive accountability tests? Who really cares about students' attitudes, interests, or values?

Those are good questions, and the answers to them all hinge on one powerful reality. It is a reality represented graphically in Figure 9.1. As you can see in that figure, student's affective status is *predictive* of students' future behavior. That's right, if you want to predict whether students will engage in gobs of free-time reading once they leave school, you'll be able to make such a prediction more accurately if you measure those students' affect regarding reading. Although *being able to read* is surely a necessary precursor to children's choosing to read on their own, students' attitudes toward reading are a significant determiner of whether those students will actually read things they're not required to read. Students who love to read while they're in school will, on average, be the students who read on their own after school is only a memory.

And this, of course, is the reason that any really responsible educator dare not dismiss the importance of students' affect. Students' attitudes, interests, and values influence what students will do later on in life, that is, how students will

Figure 9.1 Why Students' Affect Is So Important

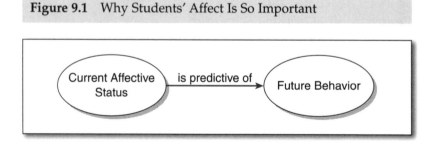

behave later on in school and later on when school is all wrapped up. If educators care about students' *future* well-being, and few educators do not, then educators must be seriously attentive to students' *current* affect.

One way of thinking sensibly about students' affect is to regard affective variables as *dispositions*. In other words, affective variables can be regarded as factors that predispose students' to behave subsequently in certain ways. Indeed, it is often useful for educators to refer to affect simply as "affective dispositions" because this is the way students' affect *works*. To illustrate, let's say that the science teachers in Harrison High School, an urban secondary school, have collaborated intensively in an effort to promote their students' positive attitude toward science as a career. Yes, the chemistry teachers, the physics teachers, the biology teachers, and the general-science teachers have worked out a series of affectively oriented activities intended to get the students in their classes to, as they say, "groove on science." Now, let's suppose that this systematic effort to have students acquire positive attitudes toward science, as well as a genuine interest in science, has worked wonderfully, that is, almost all of the Harrison High students who have taken one or more courses in science leave school with a positive affect toward science as a career. Does this mean that *all* of those youngsters will actually end up later as scientists? Of course not. Having a positive attitude toward science might *predispose* a student toward a career in science, but that's all it is, a *predisposition*. A range of real-world events will lead many of those would-be scientists toward other kinds of nonscientific careers.

Okay, let's concede that students' current affective status is not a dead-certain predictor of those students' future behaviors. Does this mean educators should have little or no interest in molding students' less-than-perfect affective predispositions? You can easily guess the right answer to that question.

To illustrate, let's say that a middle school's math teachers have gone out of their way with their school's students to engender positive attitudes toward mathematics. The teachers are fed up with the allegation that many of the school's students emerge from school with full-blown "math phobia," that is, being deathly afraid of all matters mathematical. As a consequence of these middle school's math teachers' efforts over a two-year period, however, far more students leave the middle school with a positive attitude toward mathematics than was the case just a few years earlier. Surely, those math teachers should be elated that most of their students are departing from middle school with positive dispositions toward mathematics. And, because math teachers are good at numbers, they recognize that the more students who leave school with positive attitudes toward mathematics, the more students there will be who use mathematics comfortably in later life—and the more students there will be who actually pursue advanced mathematical studies. It's just a matter of probabilities. Affective dispositions play a big role in how students subsequently behave. Educators who are oblivious of students' affect are, in most instances, shortchanging those students.

If teachers are able to get a reasonably accurate fix on their students' affect, then such teachers (1) can decide if they need to engage in any affect-influencing activities in their classes and, if they decide to do so, (2) can evaluate the success of such affectively focused instructional endeavors. As you will learn in just a moment, the evidence that teachers can obtain from their affective assessments is exclusively intended to help those teachers make instructional decisions about *a group of students,* not about an individual student. Affective assessments will not tell a teacher anything about the affective status of a particular student. Nonetheless, teachers' being able to discover the affective status of an entire class of students can contribute meaningfully to a teacher's instructional decision making—as you will soon see.

Although it's one thing to concede that students' affective status is important, it's quite another thing to figure out how to actually ascertain students' affective status. However, because this is a book about educational assessment, you'll not be traumatized to discover that we'll now turn to the *measurement* of students' attitudes, interests, and values.

Top Two Targets

When educators decide to assess their students' affect, they need to identify affective variables that can be modified. There's no sense in measuring students' affective dispositions merely because "it's interesting." So, the selection of to-be-assessed affective targets always warrants careful attention.

Not too long ago, a colleague and I decided to assess students' affect, and we spent several weeks zeroing in on what we'd finally try to measure. My colleague was Rick Stiggins who, for decades, was one of the few U.S. measurement specialists who attended with seriousness to classroom assessment—as opposed to large-scale assessment. At the time, we were both living about 10 minutes from one another near Portland, Oregon, and we were both proponents of formative assessment. We were convinced that, when properly implemented by a teacher, formative assessment or, as some prefer to label it, "assessment *for* learning," would have a substantial impact on students' affective dispositions. Accordingly, we needed to identify those affective variables that would be the focus of our yet-to-be-developed affective inventories—inventories intended to measure the affective consequence of formative assessment.

In all, we had about four meetings, each of them a few days apart, to analyze what sorts of affect *might* be influenced when formative assessment was working as it should work. We also recognized that if we were able to do a decent job in creating inventories capable of assessing the kinds of student affect apt to be influenced by formative assessment, those inventories might then serve as sensitizing instruments for teachers, that is, as instruments focusing a teacher's instructional attention on the affective outcomes of instruction.

What we finally came up with, and in so doing developed four inventories suitable for use with students in different grade ranges, were the following two affective variables: (1) *students' academic efficacy* and

(Continued)

(Continued)

(2) *students' eagerness to learn.* We thought, and still do, that if formative assessment is purring along as it should be purring, students will be more successful in what they are trying to learn and, as a consequence, will regard themselves as more capable learners. At the same time, in an appropriately structured formative-assessment classroom, students' increased successes in dealing with learning tasks will increase their eagerness to learn new things.

It takes time and some serious thinking to identify the appropriate foci for affective assessment devices. Our top two may not have been the right ones, but, after all, they were still our top two. (Rick or I will relay a set of our affective inventories to those colleagues who request them politely.)

HOW TO ASSESS STUDENTS' AFFECT

Let's set the stage for a brief look at affective assessment by supplying you with a three-attribute overview of how to conceptualize an affective-assessment strategy. Here is such a three-part strategic overview:

A Three-Attribute Strategy for Assessing Students' Affect

Affective-assessment devices should be self-report inventories, completed by students under conditions of both actual and perceived anonymity, from which only group-focused inferences— not individual-focused inferences—can be properly drawn.

If school leaders can recognize and understand the three attributes set forth in the above assessment strategy, that is, (1) the use of self-report inventories (2) that are completed anonymously and (3) which provide only group-focused inferences, then those school leaders will have acquired a defensible framework for thinking about how to measure students' affect. Let's consider, in turn, each of these three key attributes.

Self-Report Inventories

Although it is possible to assess students' affect by employing elaborate and exotic measurement procedures— for instance, using procedures involving the use of one-way observation mirrors or even by relying on assessment assistance from paid accomplices—as a practical matter such complicated assessment approaches are a pain to pull off in the day-to-day real world of schooling. What educators need, when measuring students' affect, is a low-cost and easily implementable assessment approach. In the assessment of students' affect in schools, esoteric approaches lose out. The use of *self-report inventories* can efficiently and unobtrusively supply educators with the evidence they need in order to arrive at valid inferences about their students' affect. Later in the chapter, an example will be supplied of such an inventory, and you will see there is nothing particularly complicated or off-putting about these sorts of affective assessment devices. Although deceptively simple, self-report inventories can function as potent tools to fulfill educators' affective-assessment requirements.

Typically, a self-report inventory will consist of a series of statements to which, one-by-one, the responding student indicates a particular level of agreement. To illustrate, if an affective inventory contained a statement such as "I am usually frightened when I know I must make an oral presentation to my classmates," then the responding students might be asked to indicate whether, for each such statement, they "strongly agree," "agree," "are uncertain," "disagree," or "strongly disagree." Because the statements in a self-report affective inventory are almost always phrased in both a positive *and* negative fashion, students' expressed agreement or disagreement with those statements can accurately reflect students' affective leanings.

Anonymity

When we assess students' affective dispositions, we are trying to get *an actionably accurate* estimate of those students' covert attitudes, interests, or values. That is, we are trying to get a sufficiently accurate fix on students' hidden affective dispositions so that any actions we take to address students' affect won't be too far off the mark. But, for many students, accuracy goes out the window when we ask them to identify themselves as they respond to an affective inventory. Far too many students will answer not in a way that represents their true feelings but, rather, in a "socially desirable" manner, that is, in a fashion intended to please those (in society) who will be looking at the students' responses. In most educational settings, this usually means that students who are asked to place their names on an affective inventory will often try to respond "in a way that pleases the teacher." To assess students' affect accurately, we need honest responses to affective-assessment devices, not apple-polishing responses from those students. Therefore, affective inventories must be filled out by students with complete *anonymity*, both *real and perceived anonymity*. If students don't believe their responses are absolutely *untraceable* back to them, then those students are apt to dishonestly sweeten their responses with too many splashes of social desirability. Without anonymity, many students will respond in a way they think we'd like them to respond. To minimize the likelihood of students' responses being too influenced by social desirability, anonymity in students' completion of any affective inventory is absolutely mandatory.

Here are four anonymity-enhancement procedures educators can use to ensure that a student's completion of an affective assessment inventory is totally anonymous and—just as importantly—is seen by students to be totally anonymous. First, in the inventory's printed directions, and in the teacher's oral presentation of an affective inventory, *students should be informed* that there are no right or wrong answers, and what's being sought are their anonymous, honest answers. Second, before distributing an affective inventory to students, a teacher should *supply a rationale for the assessment.* For example, teachers can explain to students that the only reason for collecting this kind of information is for *the teacher to improve instruction*—now and in the future. It should be made clear there is no interest in evaluating any individual student or in evaluating the whole class. Third, *restrict students' responses only to untraceable marks* (for instance, X marks or check marks), and tell students before they complete the inventories that they are not to write their names on the inventories *or to make any written comments.* The only kind of responses to an inventory's items should be the X marks or check marks called for in the inventory's directions. (Because some teachers may wish to ask students for additional comments, such comments can be collected—again anonymously— but on totally separate forms collected apart from the completed affective inventories.) Fourth, install some sort of *anonymous collection procedure,* and announce the nature of this procedure well in advance of students' completion of their affective inventories. For example, students might deposit their completed inventories, perhaps after folding them, in a stationary cardboard collection box or in a collection box that's passed around the room. Clearly, what the teacher is trying to do is communicate honestly that students' responses will be untraceable back to the student who completed a particular inventory. Incidentally, teachers should not be surprised if it takes several collections of anonymous affective responses before most students really accept the notion that their responses will be truly anonymous and, therefore, that unvarnished honesty is appropriate as students complete the inventories.

Group-Focused Inferences

It is particularly important for school leaders to recognize that when using anonymously completed self-report inventories with students, teachers can only make valid inference about a *group* of students. Teachers cannot make valid inferences about an *individual* student. For one thing, of course, students are completing the inventories anonymously, so unless the teacher had been dishonest when informing students that their responses would be anonymous, there's really no way a teacher can tell which student completed which inventory. But even if a teacher could somehow magically determine which responses had been supplied by which students, there still are reasons that the only legitimate inference a teacher can make should be about an entire class of students—and never about particular students in that class. What the teacher must be guided by, then, is the *average* response of a group of students to an affective inventory, for instance, based on the mean or median response of a class-full of students to such an inventory.

But, besides the anonymity problem, it must also be recognized that even if fool-proof anonymous responding mechanisms are in place, some students will still "play it safe" by answering in a way those students think the teacher would want them to answer. Thus, suppose in a mathematics class there were opportunities to agree or disagree with a statement in an affective inventory such as "I find mathematics to be really interesting." Some students, fearing that too many negative responses from students, even if anonymous, might displease the teacher, might supply a goody-goody response by strongly agreeing with the statement that mathematics is interesting. So, it seems, some students' responses—even to an anonymous inventory—will be more positive than they should be had the student been completely candid. Many classes have at least one Butter-Up Betty or Kiss-Up Clyde who wish, above all else, to keep the "all powerful" teacher positively disposed toward a class. Such too-positive students will, obviously, tend to make the *average* of students' responses to an affective inventory unwarrantedly high.

Conversely, however, some students will use the cloak of anonymity to "stick it to the teacher" by being more negative that they actually feel. These "get back at the teacher" students will tend to supply excessively negative responses to an affective inventory. Such too-negative responses will, of course, tend to lower students' average scores on an anonymous affective inventory.

Will the too-positive and too-negative responses totally cancel each other out? No, such wishful thinking rarely pans out. However, at least some degree of compensatory cancellation will occur in most situations where self-report inventories are being used to gauge students' affect. Reliance on students' average responses to form an inference about a student group's affect, therefore, surely will not yield a super-precise, "can't miss" estimate of a group's affective status. But if the accuracy of an average-based inference about a student group's affective status is on target enough to help the teacher get a reasonably accurate fix on a group's affective dispositions—then those average-based, group-focused inferences will have served their purpose.

An Oldie but Goodie

More than a quarter of a century ago, a second edition of the following book was published: *Nonreactive Measures in the Social Sciences*. Its authors were Eugene J. Webb, Donald T. Campbell, Richard D. Schwartz, Lee Sechreat, and Janet Belew Grove (1981). It was a book about how to carry out assessments in a manner that did not intrude on people's routine behaviors. It is an absolutely enthralling book because it sets forth a range of innovative ways to assess such variables as the sorts of affective dispositions in which educators are often interested.

I know that to regard a measurement book as "enthralling" casts instant doubt on the veracity of the enthrallee. A measurement books is not supposed to be "a good read." And yet, this one is. If school leaders have a hankering to dive deeper into the assessment of students' affect, they'll find this book more than a little thought provoking.

In the final analysis, however, as enticing as many of this book's clever assessment techniques are, in all but a very few laboratory schools, the kinds of assessment ploys set forth by Webb and colleagues would be too much trouble to pull off in a typical public school. But perhaps, once in a long while, certain of the assessment procedures set forth in *Nonreactive Measures in the Social Sciences* just might be a school leader's affective assessment of choice.

Building an Affective Inventory

Most of us have, more than a few times during our lives, completed a self-report inventory in which we were asked to register agreement or disagreement with a set of statements about this or that. Those inventories are usually Likert inventories named after Rensis Likert (1903–1981) who, in the 1930s, introduced a novel assessment procedure for gauging people's attitudes and values by asking them to respond to a collection of statements, some stated positively and some stated negatively, by choosing one of the following response options: Strongly Agree, Agree, Uncertain, Disagree, Strongly Disagree. Over the years, the vast majority of affective inventories have employed some variation of the Likert assessment strategy.

One problem with a genuine Likert inventory is that it is focused on a single affective variable, for instance, students' attitude toward racial groups other than their own. So, to get at such an attitude, one might use a Likert inventory of, say, a dozen or so statements—all of them focused on this single attitudinal variable. Yet, many teachers think that the administration of too many assessments, whether measuring cognitive or affective variables, takes excessive time away from instruction. Thus, because traditional Likert inventories deal with only a single affective dimension, and would require the administration of a separate inventory for each variable assessed, we increasingly find that educators who are assessing their students' affect are relying on a *multifocus Likert-like inventory* such as the excerpt presented in Figure 9.2.

As can be seen in Figure 9.2's illustrative inventory, six items taken from a 10-item affective inventory are presented. The items we see in the inventory deal with three affective variables. The other items, the ones we don't see, deal with other affective variables. Each of the three affective variables being assessed in the Figure 9.2 inventory are addressed by two statements, one positive statement and one negative statement. The three affective variable are, in turn, (1) students' "sense of academic efficacy" as assessed by Items 1 and 9, (2) students'

Figure 9.2 An Illustrative Excerpt From a Multifocus Likert-Like
Affective Inventory for Middle School Students

SCHOOL AND ME

Directions: This inventory contains a number of statements dealing with you and school. Please read each statement, and then indicate whether you *agree* or *disagree* with the statement. If you are *unsure,* then choose that response. There are no right or wrong answers, so please answer as honestly as you can. You are to answer anonymously, so do not write your name on the inventory or make any other written comments. Only make check marks as you can see in the sample below.

	Response (for each statement)		
A Sample Statement	**Agree**	**Unsure**	**Disagree**
I like watching cartoons on TV.	☑	☐	☐

After completing the inventory, please deposit it in the response box near the classroom door. When all students have turned in their completed inventories, they will be taken directly to the principal's office for tabulation. Thank you for your help.

	Response (for each statement)		
Statements	**Agree**	**Unsure**	**Disagree**
1. When I am asked to tackle a new task in my school, I usually can do it well.	☐	☐	☐
2. Most of the time, I really am uninterested in learning new things at school.	☐	☐	☐
3. I feel safe whenever I am at school.	☐	☐	☐
8. Some of the time, I really don't feel completely safe at school.	☐	☐	☐
9. When my teachers give me a new kind of assignment, I sometimes doubt I can do it.	☐	☐	☐
10. Learning new stuff at school is not something I really enjoy very much.	☐	☐	☐

"interest in learning" as assessed by Items 2 and 10, and (3) students' "perceived safety while in school" as assessed by Items 3 and 8.

Using students' sense of academic efficacy as an example, what we hope to see—when students regard themselves as academically efficacious—would be many students agreeing with Item 1 and disagreeing with Item 9. Considering that these two statements deal with the same affective variable, one statement phrased positively and one statement phrased negatively, we then assign two points when a student *agrees* with the positively phrased statement (in this example, agreeing with Item 1) and two points when a student *disagrees* with a negatively phrased statement (in this example, disagreeing with Item 9). A response of Unsure is always assigned one point. Thus, scores for an individual student's sense of academic efficacy can range from a low of zero to a high of four points.

Similarly, for the two statements dealing with each of the other affective variables being assessed by the inventory, a student's score can range from a high of four points to a low of zero points. To obtain an estimate of the affective dispositions for a whole classroom full of students, the teacher simply calculates an average (for instance, an arithmetic mean) based on all students' responses to the two items dealing with each variable.

Although a pair of items per variable will usually supply teachers with a sufficiently accurate fix on a student group's affective status, if the teacher wants to double that number of items, by using four statements per affective variable (two positively phrased, and two negatively phrased) this can be easily done.

The actual phrasing of the statements in an affective inventory is, of course, important. The statements should not be structured so that essentially no students will ever agree (or disagree) with a particular statement. Because there are so few statements per affective variable, it is important to phrase each of the statements so that a reasonable degree of variability in students' responses is likely.

You surely realize this rapid-fire peek at how an affective inventory might be built does little more than provide you with a general glimpse of what's involved when educators construct their own inventories to measure students' affect. Albeit brief, however, the description of how to build a multi-focus affective inventory was intended to show you that, while not fools' play, the construction of these sorts of affective inventories is far from rocket science. Thoughtful educators who attend to the words employed in their inventories, and are willing to revise those inventories a time or two after first using them, can usually create and employ affective inventories capable of providing valid inferences about the affective dispositions of groups of students. Such affective inference, when acted on by teachers, can enhance the quality of education provided to students.

This chapter has provided only a brief look into the nature of affective inventories and how they can be constructed. For school leaders who wish to employ such assessment tools in their own settings, additional reading about the nuts and bolts of affective assessment will surely be in order. Several Recommended Readings are cited at the close of the chapter for those school leaders who wish to learn more about the important process of assessing students' status with respect to these significant, life-influencing variables.

CRUCIAL UNDERSTANDINGS

There are really only two crucial understandings about affective assessment needed by all school leaders, and they revolve around, first, why this sort of assessment should take place at all and, second, how to go about it. If the assessment of student affect were to become a routine component of the evidence-gathering operations employed by schools, districts, or states, you can be assured that teachers would become far more conscious of the need to attend to students' affect as they carry out their instructional activities. It has often been pointed out that "we measure what we treasure." Accordingly, if we routinely begin to assess students' attitudes, interests, and values, such an assessment activity will send an unequivocal message to educators that the measurement of affect is, indeed, sufficiently important to warrant all teachers' instructional attention.

To illustrate, if a mathematics teacher has decided to administer an affective inventory about students' attitudes toward math—on a pretest-posttest basis—it is likely the teacher will, at least occasionally, think about the affective impact of his instructional activities. Anticipated assessments almost always influence current conduct.

Here, then, are the two crucial understandings about affective assessment flowing from this chapter.

CRUCIAL UNDERSTANDINGS

- Because students' affective dispositions are potent predictors of those students' future conduct, school leaders should seriously consider the possibility of routinely assessing students' attitudes, interests, and/or values.
- Students' affect should be assessed via anonymous, self-report inventories permitting only group-focused inferences about students' affect—never inferences about an individual student's affective dispositions.

RECOMMENDED READING[*]

Anderson, L. W., & Bourke, S. F. (2000). *Assessing affective characteristics in the schools* (2nd ed.). Manwah, NJ: Lawrence Erlbaum.

Likert, R. (1932). A technique for the measurement of attitudes. *Archives of Psychology, 140,* 1–50.

Webb, E. J., Campbell, D. T., Schwartz, R. D., Sechreat, L., & Grove, J. B. (1981). *Nonreactive measures in the social sciences* (2nd ed.). Boston: Houghton Mifflin.

Wilkerson, J. R., & Lang, W. S. (2007). *Assessing teacher dispositions.* Thousand Oaks, CA: Corwin.

---

* Complete bibliographic information and brief annotations are supplied for the following recommendations in the Reading Recommendations Roundup (pp. 181–190).

10

"Top 20" Crucial Understandings About Educational Assessment

L ooking back at the previous chapters' crucial under-standings regarding educational assessment—the key understandings an effective school leader ought to possess, it turns out that those understandings total up to 20. This wasn't planned. Instead, it was just that as I was trying to isolate each chapter's most important must-know things, I ended up with two or three crucial understandings per chapter, and the whole collection of those understandings added up to 20. Actually, this is fine with me. In truth, when I was growing up, it seemed many things in my world culminated in a "top 20" list. Each weekend, as a teenager, I listened to a famous radio disk jockey as he unveiled that week's top-20 most pop-ular musical hits. I always yearned to find my own favorite recordings listed among the week's most applauded music. So, because it turns out that there are 20 understandings about educational assessment that, at least in my opinion, are crucial for a really capable school leader to comprehend, I'm not distressed at all with the number 20.

Okay, because this is the wrap-up chapter in the book, how should you—the reader—deal with these 20 crucial understandings? Well, I submit that you need to take *two specific actions* regarding those understandings. First, you need to make sure you *grasp the meaning of each understanding* so well that you can effectively explain it to a colleague or, if asked, even to a layperson. Second, you actually *need to start explaining* certain of the 20 understandings to those apt to be affected by them. To repeat, you need to (1) comprehend all 20 crucial understandings and (2) explain at least some of them to others. Let's look briefly at each of these two different but important activities.

UNDERSTANDING THE UNDERSTANDINGS

Initially, you need to make sure that you really do comprehend what's involved in each crucial understanding. Later in this chapter, all 20 understandings will be listed (and numbered) in the order you encountered them in the book. The name of the chapter in which each understanding appeared is also cited. So, a straightforward way to figure out if you really recognize what's going on in each understanding is to go through the list, one crucial understanding at a time, then pretend you have been asked by someone to explain—in your own words—what's meant by that particular understanding. You might choose as your imaginary "explain to" person a colleague, that is, an educator who knows something about what goes on in school, or a layperson, such as a parent or a member of a community group who knows relatively little about what takes place in school. *I'm really asking you to do this.* Mentally, try to walk through the key elements of an explanation regarding what's meant by *each* of the 20 crucial understandings. Although these explanations will only be "going on in your head" instead of actually taking place in the real world, you may find as you try to tell an imaginary person about the meaning of a particular understanding that you have trouble doing so. If this occurs, then it's time to make one or two fix-it moves.

First, you might simply reread the sections of the relevant chapter bearing on the crucial understanding, sections that apparently induced an explanatory stumble. Sometimes a careful rereading of the relevant section of a chapter will conquer any confusion. But let's face it, the problem may be mine, not yours. I simply may not have explained adequately what's involved in a particular crucial understanding. I tried to do an acceptable job, of course, but the road to confusion is often paved with an explainer's less-than-satisfactory explanation.

Second, if a rereading of the chapter's relevant paragraphs does not enable you to explain (mentally) the meaning of any of the top-20 crucial understandings about educational assessment, then it is time to forage a bit in the Recommended Reading given at the close of each chapter. You'll recall that I've typically suggested only a handful of additional reading possibilities at the close of the chapters, and always supplied a brief annotation of those suggestions in the Recommended Reading Roundup near the book's end. Because these Recommended Readings represent either more-complete explanations of a chapter's contents (by me, but in another source) *or* someone else's take on that very same content, a quick dip into those recommended resources can often clarify whatever seems to be impeding your explanatory-level comprehension of a top-20 crucial understanding. Remember, if you don't grasp any of those understandings well enough to explain it, although only in a make believe manner, it's likely you aren't grasping this understanding with a sufficiently firm grip. By doing a bit of browsing in the sources cited as Recommended Reading, you can almost always increase your comprehension of the crucial understanding that's involved.

SPREADING THE WORD

Aristotle opined, probably when he was in an opining mood, that the most serious metaphysical evil occurs when any entity's potential is unrealized. Putting it a bit less abstrusely, Aristotle believed that whenever a person or thing possessed the capacity to become something, and did not do so, the failure to achieve this potential was inherently wrong. That is, when any capacity is not fully implemented as it might have been implemented, this is profoundly inappropriate. Well, assuming you have by now comprehended the top-20 crucial understandings well enough to be able to explain their meaning to colleagues or to laypersons, why not heed Aristotle's advice? That's right, I'm asking you to start explaining!

Not Just for Kids

Human beings are tough to change. That's true whether those human beings are little ones or big ones. So, when school leaders are asked to increase the assessment literacy of their colleagues, all of whom are grownups, and most of whom have been relatively successful in their profession, this constitutes a nontrivial challenge. Experienced educators who have been doing pretty well are unlikely to clamor for opportunities to learn more about something they don't really see as all that relevant to their work. So, it is in recognition of the realistic recalcitrance of many seasoned school people to learn about assessment that some promoters of assessment literacy will be tempted to play the *good-for-kids* card. Resist the temptation. It rarely works.

That's right, if you want to modify the entrenched behaviors of a group of educators, never tell them to do what you've suggested because "It's good for kids." Granted that most educators entered the profession because they wished to educate their society's children and, other things being equal, educators will usually subscribe to what's apt to benefit children. But it is markedly more powerful, when appealing to an experienced educator, if you can legitimately assert that "This is good for *you!*" Putting it differently, promoters of assessment literacy will be more successful if what a target educator hears is the following: "If I increase my personal understanding of educational assessment concepts, that is, if I enhance my own assessment literacy, *this will be good for me.*"

> Human beings, particularly adults, tend to act out of self-interest. So, the strategy that will best benefit children will be one that *simultaneously* is "good for kids" and also is "good for the educator involved." If school leaders really want to be successful in spreading the word, so their colleagues will understand more about educational measurement, the "word spreader" must make it clear to colleagues that *the more an educator understands about the key concepts of educational assessment, the more effective the educator is likely to be.*
>
> Fortunately, because effective, assessment-literate educators make better decisions, it turns out that children end up being better taught. So, even though arriving by the back door, educators' enhanced assessment literacy will almost certainly be good for kids!

One of the most serious problems in today's education profession is that the level of educators' "assessment literacy" is so abysmally low. As indicated in Chapter 1, many of today's crucial educational decisions are made on the basis of students' test results, yet few educators really know what's taking place when students are being tested. That's not only embarrassing—but downright dangerous. And, equally unfortunate, few laypersons—particularly parents and educational policymakers—have even a foggy notion about what goes on in the world of educational assessment. Because so few educators possess sufficient assessment acumen to relay those insights to laypersons, then laypersons tend to remain ignorant about really significant assessment considerations related to education. This pervasive lack of knowledge about educational assessment can be aptly described as *assessment illiteracy.* And there is scant doubt that assessment illiteracy can trigger seriously unsound decisions about how we educate our students.

Once you have really mastered the top-20 crucial understandings about educational assessment, *you can personally help change this.* That's right: I am suggesting—as an Aristotelian consequence of your reading this book—you have acquired a brand-new potential or, if you will, a new obligation. You really do need to spread the word, that is, you need to increase the assessment literacy of those around you. The top-20 understandings set forth in this book aren't beyond the comprehension capacities of almost anyone you know. And these crucial understandings, whether grasped by the teacher down the hall or by the person standing behind you in the grocery line, can play a role in how we educate our students.

I entreat you, therefore, please try to do whatever you can as a school leader to increase the assessment literacy of those around you. Almost all of your educator colleagues need to be aware of what's in these 20 understandings. And laypersons, whether parents, policymakers, or vanilla-variety citizens will, on occasion, have a need to know what's meant by certain of these important assessment concepts. The 20 crucial understandings identified in this book are far too important to keep to yourself.

THE TOP-20 LIST

Here, then, are the 20 crucial understandings about educational assessment that were addressed in the preceding chapters. Do whatever you can to comprehend and internalize them. Remember, if you have trouble coping with any of them, scurry back to the originating chapter or to that chapter's Recommended Reading.

Chapter 1. Why Do We Test?

1. Educators use assessment-elicited evidence about students' covert knowledge, skills, and affect to make inferences that can then contribute to more-defensible educational decisions.

2. Although it is widely believed that large-scale educational tests are remarkably accurate, they are much less precise than is thought.

Chapter 2. Validity: Assessment's Cornerstone

3. Three professionally sanctioned varieties of evidence are collected, depending on an educational test's

measurement mission, to support the validity of test-based inferences—rather than the validity of the tests themselves.

4. Because most educational assessments are used to determine whether students have mastered a set of curricular aims, educators must be particularly attentive to the quality of any alignment studies supplying content-related evidence of validity.

Chapter 3. Test Reliability

5. Test reliability refers to the consistency with which a test measures what it is measuring, but the three professionally accepted types of reliability, that is, stability, alternate-form, and internal consistency, represent fundamentally different ways of looking at a test's measurement consistency.

6. A test's reliability is usually reported either as a correlation-based reliability coefficient or as the percentage of test-takers' identical classifications on different test administrations, but because internal-consistency estimates of reliability are based on a single test administration, internal consistency is reported only as a reliability coefficient.

7. A test's standard error of measurement (SEM), based on the test's variability as well as its reliability, should be employed to determine the consistency of an individual student's test performance—with smaller SEMs indicating more consistent assessment.

Chapter 4. Assessment Bias

8. Assessment bias, the qualities of a test that offend or unfairly penalize test-takers because of group-defining personal characteristics, can seriously diminish the validity of assessment-based inferences about the individuals being offended or unfairly penalized.

9. Because two strategies have been employed to identify potentially biased items in educational tests, namely, judgmental and empirical bias-detection strategies, all educators should be familiar with the general nature of each strategy.

Chapter 5. Instructional Sensitivity

10. A test's instructional sensitivity represents the degree to which students' performances on that test accurately reflect the quality of instruction specifically provided to promote students' mastery of whatever is being assessed.

11. When educational accountability tests are instructionally insensitive, they often supply misleading evidence regarding the quality of schooling and, as a consequence, foster inappropriate instructional decisions.

12. Educational accountability tests can be made more defensible by carefully attending to instructional sensitivity during the construction and review of a test's items.

Chapter 6. Test Construction

13. For constructing significant educational tests, three purpose-governed operations must be carried out: item development, item improvement, and test assembly.

14. All of the major procedures to be carried out as test items are born, polished, and packaged, can be appreciably enhanced by relying on experience-based or empirically proven guidelines that have been assembled over the years.

Chapter 7. Rubrics: Potentially Potent Evaluative Tools

15. The three essential components of a rubric, that is, a scoring guide, are (1) the evaluative criteria by which

a student's performance is judged, (2) guidance regarding how those criteria are to be used in determining the quality of a student's performance, and (3) an application strategy calling for the use of holistic scoring, analytic scoring, or a combination of both.

16. Although a skill-focused rubric can be of enormous use to educators, hypergeneral or task-specific rubrics are of limited utility.

Chapter 8. Formative Assessment: Underused Magic Bullet

17. The formative-assessment process revolves around the collection of assessment-elicited evidence regarding students' learning, such evidence then being used by teachers to make adjustments in their ongoing instruction or by students to adjust their current learning tactics.

18. Although compelling evidence shows that formative assessment will decisively improve students' learning, educators must be wary of commercially promoted programs that, though claiming to be "research-proven formative assessment," are actually imposters.

Chapter 9. Assessing Students' Affect

19. Because students' affective dispositions are potent predictors of those students' future conduct, school leaders should seriously consider the possibility of routinely assessing students' attitudes, interests, and/or values.

20. Students' affect should be assessed via anonymous, self-report affective inventories permitting only group-focused inferences about students' affect—never inferences about an individual student's affective dispositions.

A Final Word

Many factors influence how well we educate our students. But today, more than ever before in educational history, the ways in which we employ educational assessment will make our schools better or worse. Indeed, it may well be that only the amount of money we spend on schools is more important. Educational assessment is, therefore, a key element in determining the success of schooling—and the success of those who lead our schools.

Are there other things about educational assessment that a school leader can profitably know about educational assessment? Of course there are. But if you have truly comprehended the 20 understandings set forth here, you will have mastered most of what educators need to know about educational assessment. As an assessment-literate school leader, you'll be in a position to lead up a storm! Please do so.

Recommended Reading[*]

Criswell, J. R. (2006). *Developing assessment literacy: A guide for elementary and middle school teachers.* Norwood, MA: Christopher-Gordon.

Dwyer, C. A. (Ed.). (2008). *The future of assessment: Shaping teaching and learning.* New York: Lawrence Erlbaum.

Popham, W. J. (2006). *Mastering assessment: A self-service system for educators.* New York: Routledge.

Stiggins, R. J. (2008). *An introduction to student-involved assessment for learning* (5th ed.). Upper Saddle River, NJ: Prentice-Hall/Merrill.

---

[*] Complete bibliographic information and brief annotations are supplied for the following recommendations in the Reading Recommendations Roundup (pp. 181–190).

Recommended Reading Roundup

- American Educational Research Association. (1999). *Standards for educational and psychological testing.* Washington, DC: Author.

Although this set of professionally sanctioned guidelines for educational and psychological testing is slated for revision in the near future, the 1999 *Standards* govern the appropriateness of many measurement procedures carried out in connection with educational assessment. Because the *Standards* are highly influential in legal disputes regarding testing, if school leaders ever find themselves caught up in litigation based on educational assessment, acquiring a copy of the most current *Standards* would be advisable. Although seemingly technical and off-putting at first glance, the vast majority of the content contained in this important volume will be comprehensible to all school leaders—sometimes after a second, slower reading.

- Anderson, L. W., & Bourke, S. F. (2000). *Assessing affective characteristics in the schools* (2nd ed.). Mahwah, NJ: Lawrence Erlbaum.

Anderson and Bourke present a delightful second edition of a book that Anderson had written some 20 years earlier. The authors promise, after another two decades have elapsed, to tackle a third edition. What makes this book particularly relevant for those who wish to assess students' affect is its cogent argument in favor of employing self-report inventories to measure students' affect. Given the absence of many competing books dealing with this topic, the Anderson and Bourke book becomes almost a "must read" for the would-be assessor of students' affect.

- Black, P., & Wiliam, D. (1998a). Assessment and classroom learning. *Assessment in Education: Principles, Policy and Practice, 5*(1), 7–73.

When almost anyone cites the empirical evidence supporting the effectiveness of formative assessment, central in their citations will be this now-classic review of classroom-assessment research as it relates to students' learning. Commencing with almost 700 published studies dealing with a wide range of learners and a wide range of subjects, the reviewers culled out about 250 of the most rigorously conducted investigations, then proceeded to conclude that formative assessment, in a whole host of implementations, meaningfully improves students' learning. Given the mélange of diverse studies with which two reviewers had to deal, this important review is made all the more useful because of Black and Wiliam's transparency, candor, and good sense in recounting how they dealt with nontrivial methodological differences in the studies reviewed.

- Black, P., & Wiliam, D. (1998b). Inside the black box: Raising standards through classroom assessment. *Phi Delta Kappan, 80*(2), 139–148.

This oft-cited article in a widely circulated U.S. journal by two British researchers is frequently identified as the chief catalyst for American educators' interest in formative assessment. Drawing heavily on an earlier research review (Black & Wiliam, 1998a), this analysis sets forth a collection of school-reform recommendations focused chiefly on how classroom assessment can be employed to dramatically improve students' achievement. Because this *Kappan* article was well known to many American educators by the time the No Child

Left Behind Act had been signed into law (in early 2002), many U.S. educators attempted to implement the advice proffered in this influential essay to cope with the accountability sting of this new federal statute.

- Criswell, J. R. (2006). *Developing assessment literacy: A guide for elementary and middle school teachers.* Norwood, MA: Christopher-Gordon.

As its title indicates, this is a book written chiefly for elementary and middle school teachers. Nonetheless, if a secondary school teacher were to surreptitiously dip into its full-range treatment of key assessment issues, such a teacher would not be permanently scarred. Criswell does a nice job in 16 chapters of laying out many of the assessment-related topics today's school leaders will surely bump into on a sometimes-daily basis. He sets out the goals for each chapter at a chapter's outset, thereby permitting the reader to decide which chapters are of particular relevance.

- Crooks, T. (1988). The impact of classroom evaluation practices on students. *Review of Educational Research, 58*(4), 438–481.

In this excellent analysis of research related to evaluation practices on students, Crooks spends substantial time on the impact of routine classroom assessment practices as well as the motivational consequences of certain forms of classroom testing. As the Crooks' review is often cited, along with reviews by Black and Wiliam (1998a) and Natriello (1987), to support the use of formative assessment, school leaders who wish to become especially well grounded in the empirical underpinnings of formative assessment would be well advised to spend some time with Crooks' thoroughgoing review.

- Dwyer, C. A. (Ed.). (2008). *The future of assessment: Shaping teaching and learning.* New York: Lawrence Erlbaum.

This book is a collection of essays based on the authors' presentations at an invitational conference sponsored by the

Educational Testing Service. As the title of the book implies, the glue that holds the book together is a preoccupation with the ways assessment can influence both instruction and learning. Dwyer not only did a first-rate job in getting leading assessment specialists to take part in the project, but also in obliging them to remain attentive to the instructional and learning payoffs of diverse assessment incarnations.

- Glickman-Bond, J., & Rose, K. (2006). *Creating and using rubrics in today's classrooms: A practical guide.* Norwood, MA: Christopher-Gordon.

This is a useful resource for school leaders who wish to become adroit in the use of rubrics. The authors provide a wide array of illustrative rubrics and spend plenty of time in explaining how to generate one's own rubrics. A position is taken in the book that rubrics are scoring and grading tools capable of *guiding instruction, involving students,* and *informing teachers, students, and parents.* A number of additional rubric-relevant resources are presented in this practitioner-oriented volume.

- Heritage, M. (2010). *Formative assessment: Making it happen in the classroom.* Thousand Oaks, CA: Corwin.

Revolving around the everyday world of the classroom, this book was written specifically for teachers and for those who support teachers. The book's focus is on making formative-assessment practice an integral part of any classroom—at any grade level and in any subject. Written by an educator who possesses substantial experience, as both a classroom teacher and a supervisor of teachers in the United States and the United Kingdom, the book presents a remarkably practitioner-friendly set of guidelines and insights regarding formative assessment. Happily, this volume supports both the interests of educators who are beginning to explore the adoption of formative assessment as well as those of educators who can use Heritage's understanding of classroom realities to refine their formative-assessment knowledge and skills.

- Linn, R. L., Miller, D., & Gronlund, N. E. (2008). *Measurement and assessment in teaching* (10th ed.). Upper Saddle River, NJ: Prentice-Hall.

This classic measurement textbook has been a staple in educational assessment courses through the years. School leaders will find that it treats almost any fundamental topic of assessment they care about—and treats it well.

- Likert, R. (1932). A technique for the measurement of attitudes. *Archives of Psychology, 140,* 1–50.

What's particularly interesting about this seminal description of a way to assess people's affective dispositions is that the measurement challenges facing Likert three-quarters of a century ago seem to be the very same ones facing educators today who would like to get an assessment fix on their students' affect. This article, given its immense impact over the years on the assessment of attitudes, is an indisputable classic.

- Marzano, R. J. (2008). *Vision document: Getting serious about school reform, three critical commitments.* Bloomington, IN: Marzano Research Laboratory.

In this analysis, one of America's most respected commentators on the potential impact of empirical research on schooling argues that three crucial commitments must be made for school reform to properly flower, (1) development of a system of individual student feedback at the district, school, and classroom levels; (2) ensuring effective teaching in every classroom; and (3) building background knowledge for all students—particularly those with educationally challenging backgrounds. This document describes the key phases associated with each of these three commitments. Marzano's vision of what needs to happen is well worth considering, even though I quibble with this pamphlet's advocacy of hypergeneral rubrics.

- McMillan, J. H. (Ed.). (2007). *Formative classroom assessment: Theory into practice.* New York: Teachers College Press.

This is a collection of essays by leading assessment authorities dealing with basic questions related to the theory and practice of formative assessment. Although some of the book's essays are more academic than practical in tone, the book nonetheless contains a set of insightful commentaries by first-rate measurement specialists. McMillan's edited volume dealing with this topic was one of the first books focusing exclusively on the formative-assessment process.

- McMillan, J. H. (2008). *Assessment essentials for standards-based education* (2nd ed.). Thousand Oaks, CA: Corwin.

The delightful thing about McMillan's second edition of this book is that it addresses key assessment topics, but not at an excessive level of detail. McMillan recognizes that certain assessment topics can be treated at a blah, blah, blah level of analysis, but he usually gets by with a single blah. His slant on many of the topics treated in the book you are currently reading is similar, but McMillan sets a context in which there is a focus on standards-based education. This practical book can be easily read by busy school leaders. Several chapters are especially worthwhile because they are charmingly succinct.

- Mueller, J. (2009). *Assessing critical skills.* Columbus, OH: Linworth.

One might think that a book dispensed by a publisher who specializes in providing professional development resources for K–12 library media and technology specialists would not be applicable to the run-of-the-classroom teacher. But this book most definitely is. Mueller addresses with considerable clarity the challenge of how to design assessments that actually measure the critical skills so badly needed by today's students. This is not a theory-only book about the creation of assessments to assess students' mastery of high-level cognitive outcomes. On the contrary, Mueller provides a collection of hands-on tips that any teacher will find useful. This slender volume is loaded with guidelines, strategies, and real-world examples. For school leaders inclined to splash about in the test-development soup, this book is a serviceable spoon.

- Natriello, G. (1987). The impact of evaluation processes on students. *Educational Psychologist, 22*(2) 155–175.

This review of research is organized around an assessment-cycle framework containing the following categories: certification, selection, direction, and motivation. Because this review is frequently lumped together with the research reviews of Black and Wiliam (1998a) and Crooks (1987) as empirical support for formative assessment, a school leader who really wishes to dig deeply into the research rationale for the formative-assessment process might wish to explore this review, now more than two decades old.

- Popham, W. J. (2006). *Mastering assessment: A self-service system for educators.* New York: Routledge.

This collection of 15 booklets, each of which addresses a different assessment topic, was designed for use as part of a professional-development initiative to enhance educators' assessment literacy. The boxed, color-coded set of booklets was intended to be placed in a school's faculty lounge, thereby allowing teachers and administrators to complete any of the "one-sit read" booklets in which they are interested.

- Popham, W. J. (2008). *Transformative assessment.* Arlington, VA: Association for Supervision and Curriculum Development.

Because the professional association (ASCD) that published this volume made it one of their organization's "member books," well over 125,000 copies have been distributed, thus making it likely for you to encounter a colleague who may have read all or parts of it. This ASCD book treats the formative-assessment process similarly to how it was treated in the book you have almost finished reading.

- Popham, W. J. (2009). *Unlearned lessons: Six stumbling blocks to our schools' success.* Cambridge, MA: Harvard Education Press.

In this analysis, the author (me) describes six mistakes made by educators in years past—but mistakes that continue to be made today. One of those mistakes is policymakers' reliance on instructionally insensitive accountability tests to evaluate the success of our schools. Another unlearned lesson is our failure to assess students' affect, and another stems from educators' abysmal levels of assessment literacy.

- Popham, W. J. (2011). *Classroom assessment: What teachers need to know* (6th ed.). Boston: Pearson.

Written chiefly for classroom teachers and those who supervise classroom teachers, this widely used textbook, written by yours truly, treats in more detail many of the topics considered in the book you are currently reading. I could tell you more about the book's merits, but I don't like to get too gushy.

- Reeves, D. (Ed.). (2007). *Ahead of the curve: The power of assessment to transform teaching and learning.* Bloomington, IN: Solution Tree.

Doug Reeves has corralled an excellent collection of writers to join him in dealing with a host of issues regarding the relationship between testing and teaching or, more accurately, between assessment and students' learning. In turn, individual authors serve up one or more chapters related to classroom assessment, system-level assessment, assessment challenges, and assessment leadership. School leaders will not be ill served by spending some hours with this anthology.

- Stiggins, R. J. (2008). *An introduction to student-involved assessment for learning* (5th ed.). Upper Saddle River, NJ: Prentice-Hall/Merrill.

Even though Stiggins treats the conventional collection of measurement "truths" in this textbook, it focuses dominantly on how classroom teachers can employ assessment to benefit students' learning. Stiggins definitely stresses the importance of assessment quality, but he does so while promoting the instructional merits of assessment *for* learning as opposed to the more traditional assessment *of* learning that we have seen emphasized for eons. In this popular text, the author emphasizes the crucial need to meaningfully involve students in all phases of the classroom-assessment process.

- Stobart, G. (2008). *Testing times: The uses and abuses of assessment.* New York: Routledge.

In this delightful book, a prominent British professor tackles a collection of thorny assessment-related issues that seem to be as vexing in the United Kingdom as they are in the United States. Stobart tells us that assessment definitely molds how we see ourselves and, for certain, influences how we learn. He deals with prominent uses of testing including (1) IQ and ability testing, (2) multiple intelligences and emotional intelligence, (3) learning styles, (4) accountability testing and credential seeking, and (5) formative assessment. It is always useful to have friends from foreign lands share their perceptions with us regarding issues of import in our own country. Stobart's thought-provoking look at his nation's assessment scene does just that—provoke thought.

- Thorndike, R. M., & Thorndike-Christ, T. (2010). *Measurement in psychology and education* (8th ed.). Boston: Pearson.

A long-time classic textbook in the field of tests and measurement, this book touches all the typical bases in educational assessment. Worth the price of the volume all by itself is the book's preface, in which the senior author pays tribute to his father (Robert L. Thorndike) who wrote its first edition in 1955 and to his own daughter who, from this point forward, will be guiding the book's future editions.

- Webb, E. J., Campbell, D. T., Schwartz, R. D., Sechreat, L., & Grove, J. B. (1981). *Nonreactive measures in the social sciences* (2nd ed.). Boston: Houghton Mifflin.

This is a true classic when it comes to the measurement of human beings' affective dispositions. Although many of the assessment tactics presented in the volume are not readily applicable to the in-school assessment of students' affect, the nature of some of those tactics can trigger assessment approaches that might be sufficiently practical to be used in school-based assessment of students' affect. The book is, in many ways, a delightful read.

- Webb, N. L. (2002). *Alignment study in language arts, mathematics, science, and social studies of state standards and assessment for four states.* Washington, DC: Council of Chief State School Officers.

Because the vast majority of alignment studies carried out in the United States during the past decade have employed Webb's procedures as set forth in this volume, any school leader who wishes to become well versed in determining the alignment among curriculum, instruction, and assessment would be well served to consult this influential analysis of how to collect content-related evidence of validity.

- Wilkerson, J. R., & Lang, W. S. (2007). *Assessing teacher dispositions.* Thousand Oaks, CA: Corwin.

Although this book deals with teacher dispositions rather than student dispositions, three of its chapters are particularly applicable to the measurement of students' affect. Chapter 1 provides an excellent explanation of what dispositions are and why we should measure them. Then, Chapter 2 supplies a broad-brush view of measurement methods that can be employed to assess dispositions. Finally, in Chapter 5, we encounter a nice nest of nuts and bolts dealing with the creation of actual instruments to assess affect. If your only focus is on the assessment of *students'* affect, you might need to think a bit about how to apply some of Wilkerson and Lang's suggestions to such assessment, but only a bit.

Index

CORWIN

A SAGE Company

The Corwin logo—a raven striding across an open book—represents the union of courage and learning. Corwin is committed to improving education for all learners by publishing books and other professional development resources for those serving the field of PreK–12 education. By providing practical, hands-on materials, Corwin continues to carry out the promise of its motto: **"Helping Educators Do Their Work Better."**